actice series: 12 # Good-enough parenting

a framework for assessment

edited by Margaret Adcock and Richard White

Published by
British Agencies for Adoption & Fostering
11 Southwark Street
London SE1 1RQ

January 1985
Reprinted 1987, 1990
ISBN 0 903534 57 6
ISSN 0260-0803

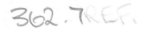

66261

Acknowledgements

This collection of papers was previously published as part of BAAF's training pack *In touch with parents* in October 1984. The editors and publishers are grateful to the following contributors: Arnon Bentovim and Liza Bingley (paper 4), Christine Cooper (paper 5) and Robin Wratten (paper 6);
and to the following authors and publishers, for giving permission for their work to be included: Vera Fahlberg (paper 7), Michael Wald and Pergamon Press Ltd. (paper 3), Her Majesty's Stationery Office (paper 8) and Norman A Polansky and Chicago University Press (paper 9).

Contents

Introduction

Courts and local authorities are continually required to make decisions about children and their families. Should a child remain with its own family or should a local authority intervene; should a child return to its natural parents or be placed in a new family; should parental rights be terminated either temporarily or permanently? All these decisions necessitate a judgement about the quality of parenting – is it good enough? The criteria that are used, however, are often not explicit. Professionals have their own standards based on a combination of values, knowledge and case law but these standards are not usually shared. They are not clearly described in text books on the law, medicine or social work. It is uncertain whether there is any consensus of professional opinion about a minimum sufficiently good level of parenting. Consequently parents and children who come under professional scrutiny are very much at a disadvantage. Parents do not know how they will be judged or what they can challenge. It is often unclear what changes they have to make for standards of care to be acceptable.

When BAAF was funded to produce training materials on working with parents to prevent their children being in long-term care, we decided that assessment must form the basis of the work and that our criteria should be explicit and clearly spelt out. We wanted to know first whether it was possible to obtain a consensus of professional opinion to which we could refer. We decided therefore to hold a small inter-disciplinary seminar with the theme 'Can we assess good-enough parenting and, if so, how?'

At the seminar many issues were raised, illustrating the complexity of making assessments and decisions. There was discussion about the impact of professional intervention and the question of whether services are good enough, both of which must be looked at when an assessment is made. There was an awareness that it is as difficult to admit that an intervention has failed as it is to accept that treatment resources were unavailable or insufficient from the start. We also need to ask ourselves and families what is good-enough assessment. Who should do assessments and where? How should outside experts be involved? How much allowance should be made for the stressful impact of an interview with experts who are also strangers? How useful is it to make judgements on parents performing under stress?

It was suggested that two different standards are used in deciding whether to remove children from home and whether to return them to their parents. Standards are higher in the latter case because parents may have to cope with problems in the child caused by the impact of separation. It seemed useful to consider whether parenting was 'bad enough' to warrant removal from home and 'good enough' to return the child subsequently.

What emerged from the seminar was considerable agreement about the important issues in child development and parenting. It was agreed that measurement of physical development in young children was a good indication of satisfactory or unsatisfactory progress but that emotional abuse was much harder to describe and define. The difficulty for participants lay in agreeing the point at which parenting was bad enough to warrant removing the child or not good enough to allow the child to return home.

This must in part have reflected the fact that an assessment has to be based on a number of factors related to the child, the parents and the professional interventions. The combination of worrying aspects will be different in each case. For example, one child may come from a family who appears to be well supported in the community and normally functions satisfactorily, and where a single very serious injury to the child appears to have been precipitated by a sudden severe stress in the family. In another family a child may be physically well cared for but have been rejected, denigrated and criticised from birth by parents who themselves have long-standing personal and marital problems. Both families react differently to professional intervention.

In addition, as we were reminded at the seminar, there is a broader social dimension to any decision. Government and society have to decide what level of parenting is unacceptable. Decisions have to be taken or validated by the courts and they are likely to reflect a blend of both professional and political opinion.

At the end of the day participants were agreed that it would be valuable to produce a publication which would contain a framework for assessment, identifying the questions each profession should ask and providing aids for observation and information gathering. This would be an explicit structure for assessment and decision-making with criteria which could be shared with families, with other professions and with the courts.

This publication contains a summary of points to be included in an assessment, the four papers which were presented at the seminar and were subsequently slightly amended, a fifth paper by Robin Wratten written as a response to the seminar, and observation checklists, developmental charts and level of living scales produced by Vera Fahlberg, Mary Sheridan and Norman A. Polansky. We hope they will help all professions to make better decisions for children and families.

Margaret Adcock
Richard White

Assessment: a summary

Introduction

1 A good assessment is an essential basis for planning work with parents to prevent children from entering or remaining in long-term care.

2 Our model of assessment places as much emphasis on detailed observation of individuals and of family interaction as on verbal communication. Through observation you are likely to see the problems enacted before you.

3 Assessment needs to be done *with* and not *to* a family if some common understanding and agreement is to be reached about what the problems are that need resolution. One research study showed that when children come into care, the parents, children and social workers each had a different understanding of what it was that led to the separation (Wandsworth, 1979). Differing perceptions of problems do not form a helpful basis for planning work to achieve change.

It is important that time is spent initially with families to get their agreement to participate in the process and to give them some understanding of what is involved. Without this it may be difficult to assess their willingness and their ability to work towards change.

The processes of an assessment and the criteria which are used also need to be shared with parents. Some agencies are now examining the possibility of standardising their assessment procedures and the criteria they use to decide whether or not parenting is 'good-enough' for a child to remain in or return to a family. A standardised procedure has the advantage of avoiding excessive reliance on the individual social worker's knowledge and values and makes it more possible for parents to understand what is happening.

4 In an assessment we should identify and share with the family the following aspects of the situation:
- the problem areas for the child or his upbringing which cause us and the family concern
- the environmental factors which contribute to the problem
- aspects of the individual functioning of the child and other family members which contribute to the problem
- the level of parental and family functioning
- aspects of the family history that may be relevant to the situation
- the potential for change
- the changes that are necessary to resolve the problem

Problem areas which cause concern

An assessment may be called for in two different situations. It may be that the family has asked us for help with problems concerning a child or his or her upbringing. Alternatively, a social worker or other agency may have suggested that there is a problem within the family which gives cause for concern and which could lead to a child entering or remaining in long-term care. It is essential to be clear at this stage why the problem is a cause for concern and to ask what are the likely consequences if the problem continues.

For the child who remains with his or her parents in an abusive or neglectful environment, the effects may range from death to other forms of physical damage, deprivation and dwarfism through to delays in cognitive development and learning capacity and emotional problems.

On the other hand, although the child who grows up in long-term care may be in a physically safe environment, he or she may be at risk of psychological harm because of the number of changes of placement experienced or the inability to form secure attachments or because long-term residential care may affect the child's ability to function in later life as a good parent. A team approach to assessment is extremely useful. If workers making an assessment do not know what the long-term consequences of a particular problem may be, colleagues from other disciplines (such as paediatrics, child psychiatry and educational psychology) may well be able to give them the relevant information.

Environmental factors

The importance of environmental factors cannot be overlooked. As the case below shows, relieving an environmental stress can cause immediate improvement in many areas of family life:

A single parent family consisting of the mother and four children (Ruth 14, Philip 10, Betty 9 and Alan 8) were referred for assessment because it was feared the mother would have another nervous breakdown – she had received psychiatric treatment in the past. The housing was bad and the family lived on supplementary benefit. Ruth had been cautioned by the police for shop-lifting and her mother was afraid to let her out in the evenings because the temporary accommodation was in the red-light area.

On visiting, further difficulties were presented. Philip banged his head against the bedroom wall at night and rocked the bed so violently that at times it collapsed and at the least woke his siblings (Betty and Alan) who shared the bedroom. Alan wet the bed every night. The mother complained of the house. It was unmodernised temporary accommodation: a terraced house having access immediately on to the street; three up and two downstairs rooms, with the kitchen off. The only water supply was in the kitchen and water was heated there by a small gas heater. There was no bathroom, and an outside toilet.

Upstairs the mother and Ruth shared one bedroom, Philip, Betty and Alan the other, whilst the third over the kitchen was unusable because of penetrating damp. The agreed object of the intervention was re-housing. It took five months of negotiations with the council for the family to be offered a three-bedroomed modern centrally heated home with open spaces and play areas. Ruth was allowed out at night: there was space to have friends in and for play without crowding each other out. The mother's anxiety ceased. Alan never once wet the bed again. For Philip a divan bed was obtained; its legs were unscrewed and it was put in the middle of the floor. Philip was told that he could rock as much as he liked as it was all right to do so and it would not disturb anyone. This simply died away. (Leicester Family Services Unit, 1981).

Many of the families whom social workers meet suffer from environmental and economic poverty. It is often this poverty which causes family problems to become so devastating in their consequences. Coffield et al (1981), quoted in Miller and Cook (1981), write:

'To miss the compelling force of external circumstances on the performance of the roles of parent or child, and to imagine that the fragile household is not responsive to, and sometimes even torn apart by, the pressures of poverty, unemployment and insecurity, is to attribute to poor people a freedom of choice and a control over their lives which does not stand up to enquiry.'

However, acute complexity arises because of the interaction between external and internal stress. Philp (1963), quoted in Miller and Cook (1981), says,

'Unemployment, bad housing and poverty are real impediments to happy family life and for parents such as these, they provide confirmation of feelings of failure and unworthiness...Their social situation places them in a position which re-activates or confirms their feelings about themselves in relation to those who have what they lack and have the power to give or deny them the things they need.'

There is no law which prescribes or predicts the particular effect of that interaction on a family.

Aspects of individual functioning

Standardised observations of the child's development and of changes in his or her emotional responses over time are essential. Methods of assessing these include:

- sequential measure of height, weight and head circumference
- child development schemata, eg Mary Sheridan's and Vera Fahlberg's checklists (pages 96 and 91) which cover developmental areas and the state of attachment to significant figures
- longitudinal cognitive testing, including the assessment of speech, language and play
- regular observation of the child's performance in school or nursery
- regular observation of the emotional status of the child
- Polansky's 'maternal characteristics' scale which can aid the assessment of parenting capacity in mothers (page 112)

The level of parental and family functioning

The 'level of living' provided for the child can be assessed with the help of Polansky's scale (page 108).

Present family functioning can be assessed with the Family Health Scales (see Arnon Bentovim's article, page 45). These scales look at key areas of family interaction and competence.

It is also valuable to observe the way the family performs interactional tasks. It is important to see parents performing both caring tasks (such as feeding, bathing, reading, cuddling and playing with children) and also controlling tasks where parents need to discipline their children or get them to behave in certain ways. It is useful to watch the family at work together, for instance, working on one task such as building a tower of bricks.

Try to get the family to show an example of the problem. If, for example, a mother complains that her child is unmanageable, the worker can ask the mother what behaviour would provoke a conflict. For example, the mother might say that the child would disobey and cause a row if asked to come and sit down on a chair. If the mother is prepared to demonstrate the problem by asking the child to come and sit down, this may give the worker an opportunity to observe directly how the child behaves and the parents react.

Aspects of the family history

The family history and its significance can be discovered by:
- discussion with individuals, including the family, other professionals and caretakers
- observing the way family members describe the past and the meaning they have attached to events. Bentovim and Gilmour (1981) suggest that this enables us to identify the meanings which are held in common and also the lack of common meanings which can result in conflict.

The potential for change

The following factors should be considered:
- the parents' willingness to admit there is (or was) a problem
- the parents' willingness to work towards change
- the parents' ability to ask for help and to use support systems
- the agency's willingness and ability to offer appropriate help to parents, children and (where the child is in care) to substitute caretakers. Appropriate help includes material resources and support systems, such as day care, helping parents and children to acquire new skills and behaviour, counselling and personal support.

Testing a family's motivation and ability to change is an important part of the assessment process. You want to see whether they can, with assistance, acquire new skills and behaviours or eliminate undesirable behaviours. In your meeting with a family it is useful to see whether they can, with your help, do something differently. For example, they could encourage a child to do what he is told by making a point of noticing and praising something positive the child has done.

The changes that are necessary to resolve the problem

Change should be directed at problems which have a specific effect on the child and the parents' ability to care for him or her. The parents must know what changes are needed. Stein, Gambrill and Wiltse (1978) suggest that the following questions need to be asked:
- What would have to be different before the child could remain at home or could return home?
- How would someone recognise this difference?
- Do parents have any personal problems that have to be resolved before the child could return home?
- How would things be different if these were resolved?
- What would an observer see if these differences occurred?

They also suggest that changes should be identified in relation to one

of the following outcomes:
- the acquisition of new skills and behaviours
- an increase in desirable behaviour
- the decrease or elimination of undesirable behaviour
- the maintenance of desired behaviour at a certain rate or the variation of a behaviour

References

Bentovim A and Gilmour L
(1981) 'A family therapy interactional approach to decision making in child care, access and custody cases'. *Journal of Family Therapy* 3 65-78.

Leicester Family Service Unit
(1981) *Solving family problems: a statement of theory and practice.* Leicester Family Service Unit.

Miller J and Cook T (eds)
(1981) *Direct work with families.* Social Work Practice in FSU.

Stein T J, Gambrill E D and Wiltse K T
(1978) *Children in foster homes: achieving continuity of care.* New York: Praeger Publishers.

Wandsworth, London Borough of
(1979) 'In care in North Battersea.' Draft (unpublished) report.

Assessing parenting: the context

Margaret Adcock

Margaret Adcock is a social work consultant and teaches the Advanced Course in Social Work with Children and Families at Goldsmith's College. She was formerly Principal Adviser, Education and Development at BAAF.

Very few parents meet the needs of their children all the time but the majority of parents in our society would appear to provide 'good-enough' parenting for their children in that they do not seriously prevent or hinder their children's development.

Whether we can define 'not good-enough' parenting and if so, how, is a question that in the last few years has aroused bitter disagreements, confusion and uncertainty. This would appear to be largely because of the consequences that may flow from a decision that the parenting of a specific child is 'not good-enough'.

The controversies surrounding definitions of 'not good-enough' parenting assume a particular force if the consequence is to be permanent separation of parent and child enforced by the state. The evidence suggests that state intervention is increasing; more children are being removed from home through the courts, more children are being placed for adoption against their parents' wishes and more children are being made the subject of wardship proceedings to resolve disputes about access and custody. It is difficult to know whether this reflects an implicit raising of standards about what constitutes adequate day-to-day parental care or whether it is a recognition that new decisions have to be taken early on, rather than after a long period of drift and uncertainty. The end result, however, is that in many cases the decision about whether a parent should retain the right to care for his child is taken by the state rather than by the parent himself as a result of inaction or rejection over a period of years. It would seem inevitable that this should give rise to conflict and should focus attention on the question of how 'good-enough' parenting is defined.

Although the courts have to make decisions, the legislation at present provides no detailed definitions of what constitutes inadequate parenting. Lord Justice Ormrod (1974) has suggested that in such circumstances the courts evolve rules of practice or guidelines in order to cope with the uncertainty and large potential for inconsistency. Guidelines subtly alter the question for decision.

'What is right or just?' becomes 'Is this case within or without the guidelines for practice?' This question can be answered much less subjectively but the quality of the guidelines becomes of crucial importance to the validity of decisions.

It is arguable, however, that although the courts and local authorities may have evolved guidelines, these are not explicit and the result is that there is considerable feeling that some decisions are neither right nor just. There would seem to be an urgent need to establish explicit guidelines which are widely acceptable and respected.

In my view, it will be difficult to devise guidelines which are widely acceptable if these are only concerned with the assessment of parent-child interaction at a particular point in time and ignore the potential of professional intervention both to improve or to make a situation worse. I will argue that making decisions about the point at which parenting ceases to be 'good-enough' and about what should happen to the child involves (except in very few extreme cases) consideration of a sequence of events and an analysis of the role of the professionals as well as the parents.

Assessment that the nature and quality of care provided by a parent for a particular child is 'not good-enough' is the first step. This is followed by an offer of professional intervention. The next step in certain cases may be a decision that a child should be removed from home or not returned home from care. Finally, it may be concluded that the separation should be permanent and the child should either be adopted or remain in long-term care with little or no access by the parents. At each stage in the sequence there is a need for the gathering of evidence and a detailed analysis of the facts. There is also a need to share both the information and the conclusions derived from this with the parents. This gives them an opportunity both to provide alternative explanations and an impetus to work towards change.

At the moment, conflict often arises because steps in the process are missed out and because little attention is paid to the role of the professionals: assessments are made without gathering detailed evidence; children are separated from their parents without prior professional intervention to change a situation and final decisions about long-term plans are made as a result of situations which have been created as much by professionals as by the parents.

The aims of this paper are:
● to clarify what needs to be considered at each stage in the process I have outlined and to attempt to identify those areas where there is knowledge and some certainty and those where there is uncertainty, ignorance, or where value judgements are involved

- to define the role of the professionals and discuss the possible effects of their intervention

It is important to recognise that the process of identifying inadequate parenting and making relevant decisions involves a combination of:
- *knowledge* of the relevant theory and research in a variety of fields (including child development and the law) and knowledge of available resources
- *skills* in assessment and treatment of problematic family situations
- *recognition of the values* at a personal, professional organisational level and in society as a whole which affect both our professional judgements and those of the courts

The relationship between knowledge and values is difficult to disentangle. Values are undoubtedly influenced by, and change as a result of, new advances in knowledge about children and their development. Equally, as Ingleby (1974) points out, 'the revelations of child psychology may be as much the products of the mentality which is brought to bear on the evidence as of the evidence itself!'

It is important to be explicit about the bases of our decision-making and to acknowledge whether they derive purely from personal values or can be substantiated from professional experience or knowledge. This allows other people to understand or to challenge what is happening. In view of the gravity of the decisions, social workers, who often have the ultimate responsibility for children, surely have a duty to see that relevant knowledge and skills are utilised rather than relying on 'instinct' or on personal or bureaucratic values. There is a need for all the caring professions, but for social service departments in particular, to be far more detailed and specific about their assessments and the reasons for their decision-making than often occurs at present.

The process

Identifying the problem
The first essential is to establish that there is a problem, to define it and to be clear why the problem gives cause for concern. At this initial stage it is particularly important to be aware of the influence of personal values about child rearing. The Royal College of Psychiatrists (1982) stresses that child-rearing practice should be seen not as an ideal and needing to follow a particular pattern but in terms of being adequate for a particular child.

Concern about a child needs to be shared within and/or between the professions in order to confirm or to correct the perception of individuals. It is also important to review the factual evidence. Particularly when there is a suspicion of child abuse there can be too much concentration on feelings and impressions. Reports of cases such as the inquiry into the death of Carly Taylor suggest that the significance of vital factual evidence can be ignored (Leicestershire, 1980). In other cases families can be labelled as 'abusing' on the basis of very little evidence.

Making an assessment

There appears to be little overt disagreement about what constitutes the most important needs of children. A useful starting point in assessment may therefore be a consideration of how far the basic needs are being met. The Royal College of Psychiatrists has provided a list of needs which is very similar to those described by Kellmer Pringle (1974). They suggest the child has a need for:
- physical care and protection
- affection and approval
- stimulation and teaching
- discipline and control which are consistent and age-appropriate
- opportunity and encouragement gradually to acquire autonomy

The need for continuity and an opportunity to make stable inter-personal bonds are stressed by many writers. The Royal College of Psychiatrists suggests that in situations of multiple caretaking, attention needs to be focused on whether the attachment needs of children are being adequately met. Rutter and Madge (1976) state that 'spending the early years of childhood in an environment which does not allow the development of stable interpersonal bonds seems to increase the risks of later deficiencies in social relationships'. Harold Martin (1976) concluded that a sense of continuing impermanence was significantly correlated with emotional disturbance in children who had previously been abused.

It would appear from many studies that the significance of multiple caretaking, even before a child enters care or afterwards, is often not considered until children have had numerous placements. There is an urgent need for social workers in particular to work with parents to see that children have fewer moves.

Rutter et al (1983) state that the research findings are very consistent in the demonstration of the parenting qualities that are maladaptive for the child. The child's needs may not be met because the parents have severe matrimonial problems, a psychiatric disorder, or a number of 'conduct' problems such as drinking, promiscuity, vagrancy, minor law violations, financial difficulties, serious housekeeping deficiences. It is also suggested that the collective input of these problems reduces the parents' ability to perform at a minimum level of functioning.

Inadequate parenting may take the form of:
- *neglect:* both physical and emotional – which has been defined as situations where some or all areas of basic needs are not attended to

- *rejection:* which has been defined as implying negative attitudes and practices in relation to the basic needs. It is demonstrated by threatening or abusive communication and deliberate withholding of approval, attention and affection. A label of cruelty might be applied in some instances, particularly where belittlement, morbid teasing and constant punishment take place
- *abandonment or desertion*
- *inability to provide continuity of care* and an opportunity to form attachments

There may be no difficulty in identifying where there are serious breakdowns in parenting which are characterised by physical abuse, gross neglect, overt rejection or abandonment. The problem lies in the 'grey' cases – in defining the point at which parenting failures warrant intervention and possibly legal action to impose a separation. Particularly in such situations it is important to make a detailed assessment to establish not only that there is an identifiable problem but also that there is a connection between the child's difficulties and parental behaviour.

Although paediatricians and child psychiatrists may compile a detailed assessment and diagnosis, this would not appear to be common practice amongst social workers and is probably not routine for other professionals such as health visitors, GPs and teachers. It is a particularly serious omission on the part of social workers – which was noted in the DHSS study of children boarded out (1981) – since local authority social workers have a statutory responsibility for investigating cases where a child's development may be being avoidably prevented or impaired and for acting in loco parentis to the children in their care.

There needs to be an assessment of: the child, the parents, the family interaction, the family in relation to its environment and a recognition of the impact of external forces.

Rutter et al (1983) suggest that parenting resources need to be considered in terms of such variables as the time available for parenting, the parents' own emotional state, the presence of other life stresses and problems, the qualities of the spouse and the extent to which child-rearing is shared, the existence of satisfactions and achievements apart from parenting, the availability of adequate social supports and housing conditions.

A number of writers have provided scales or checklists for assessment purposes. Stein, Gambrill and Wiltse (1978) suggest that difficulties in providing services to families may stem from the worker's perception of the severity of a client's problems. They suggest that workers must receive training in effective methods of assessment and must focus not on parental behaviour per se but on the specific effects of parental behaviour on the child. Vague concepts such as neglect, abuse and mental illness are of little help in directing attention to appropriate interventions. They stress the need to involve the family in making an assessment and they state that in one to three interviews the worker and the client can create a problem profile. These interviews will include observation of the parent-child interaction and a visit to the home. The problems noted will include those mentioned by the clients, those in case records and court reports and those noted by the social worker. The emphasis is upon facts and observable behaviour and away from motive analyses or abstractions from behaviour, such as, 'The child is said to be jealous'.

A completed profile will include:

a) a list of problems such as financial, housing, behavioural or emotional

b) the source of identification of each problem (client, verbal report, case record, etc)

c) who is said to have the problem (the child, the parent, other)

d) an example of behaviour that defines the problem (eg a child who is said to be unmanageable refused to return home from school at an appointed hour)

e) the context in which the problem is displayed (eg does the problem occur at home or elsewhere?)

f) the date on which the problem is identified

The consequences

Once an assessment has been made, decisions about further action are required. Two factors can be seen to be of crucial importance at this stage. The first is the likely consequence if the problem continues and the second is how intervention might change the situation.

Non-intervention
Both to protect families from unnecessary intrusion and to protect children from unnecessary suffering, it would seem essential that everyone involved in making decisions, including the courts, should seek to ascertain what knowledge is available about likely consequences if the situation is allowed to continue.

It would be interesting to know how often the likely consequences of parenting failure are considered and how many of the professionals who make the decisions are either acquainted with the relevant research findings themselves or seek information from others who are. In a study of 267 children whose parental rights were assumed (Adcock et al 1983) we found that comparatively little use was made of paediatric or psychiatric assessments. No paediatrician or child psychiatrist was called to give evidence in the cases that went to court.

Jones (1977), in a review of the research findings on the consequences of both the physical and psychological damage sustained by abused children, suggests we need to ask 'for what are we saving these children and what is the quality of their subsequent life?' She concludes that 'detailed study of the phenomenon of child abuse forces us to consider uncomfortable issues relating to the status and treatment of children in the population at large. Regardless of whether they have been physically abused, many children who may never come to professional attention are living in sub-optimal environments and experiencing the kind of inadequate parenting which could permanently impair and disrupt their development.'

The research findings make it clear that after a diagnosis has been made that parenting is inadequate, any decision about intervention should be based on the necessity to provide a more favourable environment within a short space of time and must include arrangements to monitor improvements. It is clear that the continuation of an unfavourable environment can perpetuate the damaging effects of earlier experiences. Jones quotes Martin and Beazley, for example, who noted that four to five years after abuse, psychiatric symptoms in children were significantly correlated with environmental factors such as the impermanence of the subsequent home, instability of the family with whom the child was living, punitiveness and rejection by caretakers and the emotional state of the parents or parent surrogate. It would appear, however, that some children are left for long periods in environments that remain unchanged or continue to deteriorate. Morse et al (1970), in a follow-up study of 25 abused children, reported that in the subsequent three years one third of the children were reinjured.

In our study of the assumption of parental rights we noted that 'efforts at prevention or at repeated rehabilitation could result in some children experiencing considerable change, disruption and very adverse home circumstances' with the result that they might subsequently be very difficult to help. An illustration of this was the case of three sisters:

'The family history of these three girls has been one long round of parental separation, changes of address, homelessness, living with relatives, and change of school. During the ten years of the parents' marriage, they have separated six times. The mother has had three prison sentences for prostitution. The children have been in care on three occasions; first following a place of safety order when the children were found unattended and badly neglected in the house; second, following allegations that the eldest daughter was being used for prostitution; and third, when they were received into care after their father had deserted the family and the mother had been sent to prison. The children have had no consistent routine in their lives and due to their unkempt and unusual appearance they have been frequently excluded and teased by other children. The eldest girl (aged 12) is already quite precocious sexually. She frequently talks to herself in unintelligible language and needs a psychiatric assessment. It is anticipated that she may present some difficulties for the children's home in the future.'

Ultimately, the judgements which have to be made about what is a tolerable environment for a child must inevitably be, to some extent, value judgements but the less precise our knowledge about consequences the greater is likely to be the influence of value judgements in making decisions. An example of this was the case of Mary, a year-old baby girl whose mother had failed despite intensive help and support to feed her adequately. Eventually, the paediatrician became so concerned that she asked the local authority to obtain a place of safety order and commence care proceedings. The social worker said that the mother's care of Mary was clearly inadequate but she did not think it was as serious as if the mother had injured the child or totally rejected her. She therefore felt the mother should be given another chance to care for Mary. She did not ask the paediatrician what was known about the long-term consequences of malnutrition in the first year of life and so the decision was made in ignorance of the fact that undernutrition may result in both transient and permanent central nervous system damage in the very young child.

Intervention
Whilst it seems clear that inadequate parenting can have a permanent harmful effect, research findings also indicate that these effects may be mitigated if circumstances improve either within the family or by placing the child in a more favourable environment. However, social workers who may play the major part in trying to effect change often seem very unclear about the optimum methods of work. Smale, summarising the various studies of social work effectiveness quotes Parsloe's work (1978) as a description of social workers' inability to provide a professionally sophisticated service:

'Nearly all the social workers we interviewed said only that the focus of their work was an individual or a family and that the work might be short or long-term. Beyond this, social workers showed little interest or capacity to analyse their rationale for determining the frequency of contact, nor whether it took place at the client's home or in the office...Similarly, whether or not a social worker saw a family together was often determined by who was at home when he visited and not by a pre-arranged plan made with the family.'

Considerations of how change can be effected must depend on the initial assessment of the specific family and the nature and duration of their problems. Various studies have shown that families in a crisis are very open to intervention and change. Crises would include a death in the family, desertion of a spouse, loss of employment. Polansky (1981) suggests that most neglectful families, however, are usually in some sort of equilibrium or in a state of slow decline. The equilibrium reflects the clients' solutions to their problems. Any intervention that has an impact brings the family to an unknown future. The family is therefore likely to have an investment in clinging to the existing state of affairs. Resistance can be reduced when the intervention includes new gratification for the client or things that help to replace what the client would lose were he to change his way of operating. For example, if a neglectful mother who spent most of her time out with different men felt that someone in her life, such as a social worker, cared what happened to her she might be able to devote a little attention to her children rather than always to herself and her social relationships.

Family rights groups suggest that insufficient attention is paid to the debilitating effects of extreme poverty and bad housing. They point out that the parents whose children come into care are, disproportionately, socially deprived lower class people. Whilst many research studies have noted the adverse influence of economic and material problems, there is also evidence that other factors are important but are difficult to disentangle. Polansky conducted a study of low-income families in the mountains of Southern Appalachia and subsequently replicated this in metropolitan Philadelphia. He found that in each case the parents who were offering their children marginal or neglectful care had character traits differing from the norms of their communities and in ways that were surprisingly similar. Wilson (1980) in her study showed that parental supervision was the most important single factor in determining juvenile delinquency and was more important than social handicap. However, there was a very close association of lax parenting methods with severe social handicap.

It cannot be assumed that improvements in material conditions alone therefore will automatically lead to improvements in parenting functioning. The conclusions to be drawn from the research would seem to be that when there are problems in parenting and there is material deprivation, attention may need to be paid to effecting change in several areas of family functioning – material, social and psychological. Polansky suggests moreover that in working with neglecting parents, the provision of concrete services has a dual purpose. It gives immediate direct help to a family which needs it and reinforces the worker's image as helpful. Expression of a desire to help in visible concrete terms is valuable; words may be a weak vehicle for conveying good intentions.

In considering what improvements can be made it is essential to discover whether parents admit that there is a problem and are willing to work towards change. Stein, Gambrill and Wiltse (1978) found that there was more chance of children being able to return to their families if the parents were willing to enter into a contractual agreement with the social worker setting out what the goals were and what each party had to do to achieve them. If, however, parents have not participated in the assessment process and have not been made aware of the nature of the professional's concern it may be difficult to make realistic decisions about change. Stein, Gambrill and Wiltse recommend that when the original assessment profile is compiled very specific questions are discussed, in order to list the changes to be made, for example:

- What would have to be different before the child could return home?
- How would someone recognise the difference?
- Do the parents have any personal problems that have to be resolved before the child could return home?
- How would things be different if these were resolved?
- What would an observer see if these differences occurred?

For each problem listed in the profile, changes are identified in relation to one of the following outcomes – the acquisition of new skills, increase in desirable behaviour, decrease or elimination of undesirable behaviour, the maintenance of desired behaviour at a certain rate or the variation of a behaviour.

Supplementing parental care
Whether alternative supports can be used to supplement deficits in parental care must depend on a careful initial assessment which includes the attitude of the parent, the age of the child, the nature of the problem and on the availability of resources. If, for example, one of the problems is that a parent never settles in one place or in one relationship, it is likely to be difficult to supplement parenting while the child remains at home. If the child is very young when problems become apparent and there are no relatives or friends available whom the parent will allow to play a major parenting role, it seems doubtful whether caring agencies can provide compensatory care over a long period of time. It may be possible, however, to provide intensive

help over a short period of time during which the parent becomes better able to cope or the difficulties in achieving any improvement become clearer.

Two case examples may illustrate these points:

Patrick and Pauline
Patrick was ten and his sister Pauline was fifteen. The mother had a psychiatric condition for which she had occasional in-patient treatment. The father had provided good care and kept the family together until he died suddenly when Patrick was eight. The mother lived the life of a virtual recluse and refused to communicate with any welfare agencies. She had a violent temper and Patrick was frightened of upsetting her in any way. For example, he would not give her any communication from the school. Nevertheless, he was clearly attached to his mother. Although he too had a violent temper and some problems in sustaining friendships, he made good progress academically at school and his teachers felt he was coping reasonably well both socially and emotionally. The deficits in the mother's care were compensated for by devoted school staff who saw that he had medical treatment, noticed that he was short-sighted and after he was given spectacles, took him for regular checks. An excellent education welfare officer negotiated with both Pauline and an aunt who took some interest, so that Patrick had clothing grants and was able to take advantage of every facility such as school outings, holidays, etc.

Darren
Darren was born when his mother, Marie, was seventeen. She had spent much of her childhood in a series of institutions after the suicide of her mother when she was eight. Marie refused all offers of help while she was pregnant and the first two months of Darren's life were spent with his mother in a series of very temporary accommodations. Finally, Marie asked for Darren to be received into care and eventually agreed to go with him to a mother and baby home. Her inadequate care of Darren and her aggressive behaviour towards the other residents made it difficult for anyone to help her. Eventually, after a fight with a member of staff, Marie walked out and Darren came back into care. Some months later, Marie was provided with a flat of her own and married Darren's father. Darren returned home to them. Another baby was born almost immediately. The physical and emotional care of the two children continued to cause concern. There was evidence that Darren was underfed and on several occasions the children were taken to hospital in a state of extreme filth or with unexplained injuries. When Darren was nearly four, his parents finally agreed to attend a family centre daily. Shortly after this his mother brought him to the centre with very severe bruising and after a medical examination he was removed on a place of safety order. His parents subsequently agreed that it would be best for Darren to be placed for adoption.

Making decisions about separation

If a detailed assessment has been made of the problems in the parenting and the effect these have on the child, and it appears difficult to modify the problems to any extent – what should happen next? It is suggested that two issues need particular consideration:

- What would be the effect on the child of removal from home or a decision not to return him home from care?
- Can the child be supplied with substitute care which is better than that provided by his own parents?

Whatever the age of the child it is necessary to assess both the history and the quality of the attachment between the parent and the child. This provides a basis for deciding what a child could be provided with as an alternative and what would need to be done to facilitate a transfer. It also provides part of the answer as to whether a child could be supplied with anything better through substitute care.

The first question is very much age-related and is particularly relevant to children aged from upwards of eight or nine years. The work of the Robertsons (1972) and others has shown how young children attach themselves to their caretakers who become their 'psychological' parents. Older children, however, are much better able to retain the image of their parents during a prolonged absence and may find it much harder to make new attachments or to transfer loyalties. Several senior social workers have expressed concern to us about situations where the deficiences in the quality of parenting seemed so severe as to make it completely undesirable for the child to be at home but the child refused to settle in an alternative permanent placement.

It seems unclear at the moment whether many of these difficulties could be resolved by better and more prolonged direct work with the children and by allowing more parental access to the child in a new placement. The successful use of professional foster home placements or late adoption placements is, however, usually based on the child's agreement to placement. It seems inevitable that there will be some children who cannot make use of family placement and some natural parents who would be unable to maintain contact without having a destructive effect on the new placement.

There seems to be little evidence to suggest that removal from home and future plans for the child are always seen as part of a process, rather than as quite separate events. Many children come into long-term care on an unplanned basis. There is, however, considerable evidence to suggest that long-term local authority care may entail substantial risks of psychological harm. Rutter et al conclude the account of their follow-up study of a group of children who had been admitted to long-term residential care with the following statement:

'It will be appreciated that the children had been admitted to an institution to protect them from the damage of remaining with their own parents in a discordant, disruptive and malfunctioning family. Accordingly, it is chastening to realise that this policy seems to have had such a devastatingly bad effect on the young people's functioning as parents.....It raised important questions for policy and practice.'

Long-term care can only be avoided if social workers realise its dangers and work either to return children home quickly or to seek the court's sanction for the permanent termination of parental rights. As Wald (1982) points out, we are willing to remove children from their parents, to keep them away from their parents in placement and ignore the parents themselves. However, we are unwilling in law to terminate the relationships which have been terminated in fact. As a result, without protecting the parents we impair the child's chances of forming a new stable relationship.

In order to prevent professional intervention from making a situation worse, Wald suggests that local authorities should be more accountable to the courts. Where the removal of a child is recommended the agency should specify to the court the programme it will use to achieve rehabilitation or it must demonstrate why rehabilitation is not possible. The time limit to achieve rehabilitation would normally be twelve to eighteen months. The burden of proof as to why a child should not be returned is on the agency, who would have to show why a return would cause serious detriment to the child.

Such a system would be a logical conclusion to the process of assessment and decision-making I have advocated in this paper. It would place as much stress on the actions of the caring professions and their ability to promote change as it would on the actions or inactions of the parent. It would offer more protection to both children and their parents.

The need for inter-disciplinary co-operation

I would also suggest that a further protection for families would be that no one group of professionals should make major decisions on their own since they will lack the totality of knowledge and skill which are required.

The medical profession will have relevant knowledge in assessing the needs of a particular child and how far the parent is contributing to or impeding the child's development. They will also have skills in alleviating or remedying some physical or emotional problems. They will need help from other professions, however, in assessing the social and legal aspects of a problem and the remedies available.

Social workers will have relevant knowledge for assessing the social aspects and of the resources available for helping a child within or away from his family. They will need help in making a full assessment that includes the physical and emotional aspects. Both groups may need assistance from other professionals such as teachers, psychologists and health visitors who are involved with a family. The courts and legal profession will have skills in interpreting both the evidence and the relevant law but they will have to rely on other professions for assistance in assessing family situations and understanding what remedies may be available.

Inter-professional collaboration is difficult in itself since each profession has a different frame of reference, a different language and may have different values. Bacon and Farquhar (1981) have described the problems this can create in non-accidental injury case conferences, including failures in communicating essential information and confusion about where the responsibility lies for making decisions. Adcock and White (1978) have discussed the problems in communication that lawyers and social workers may experience when one profession is traditionally concerned with observable facts and the other with feelings and inference.

Collaboration involves not only communication but trust. This may be particularly difficult to establish if, as is often the case, some of the professionals lack experience or real expertise in the issues. Conflicting professional opinions and values may constitute a further serious impediment. Fox (1982) suggests for example that there is a division within the caring professions between 'the kinship defenders and the society as parent protagonists' whose views diverge on the central question of the rights of parents to custody and control of their children in relation to the right of the state to intervene in parent-child relationships. She also suggests that there are divisions between the professions and that social workers are involved in protecting children from their parents and challenging the sanctity of the blood tie, whereas lawyers sanctify the blood tie. It would seem imperative however that, despite the difficulties, more emphasis is placed on the need for inter-disciplinary co-operation.

Conclusion

In our society it is accepted that children are usually best brought up in their families of origin. The state invests considerable sums of money to achieve this. Removing children from their families on a permanent basis is regarded as an extremely serious action. The transfer of parental rights is very carefully defined and circumscribed. It is possible, however, for professionals to intervene in family situations under much less stringently defined circumstances. Their actions may result in the strengthening of family relationships and enable parenting to be 'good-enough'. Equally, intervention may lead to situations where parents and children are separated and the way is paved for a subsequent termination of parental rights through adoption.

Because any intervention can have such far-reaching consequences, the professionals should be prepared to be accountable for their actions and to ensure that they have utilised all the knowledge and skills available in their decisions. At present it would appear that it is not always acknowledged that making decisions about whether to transplant children is as skilled a process as decisions about the surgical transplant of physical organs. It is, in my view, essential first to establish the role of the professionals and to clarify the process involved in making decisions about families. This provides the necessary basis for more detailed discussion and definition of when parenting is not 'good-enough'.

References

Adcock M and White R
(1978) *The assumption of parental rights and duties.* ABAFA.

Adcock M, White R and Rowlands O
(1983) *The administrative parent: a study of the assumption of parental rights and duties.* BAAF.

Bacon R and Farquhar I
(1981) 'Problems in the social work management of child abuse cases' paper given at the Third International Congress on Child Abuse and Neglect, Amsterdam.

DHSS Social Work Service London Region
(1981) *Children in care in London.* DHSS.

Fox L
(1982) 'Two valued positions in recent child care law and practice'. *British Journal of Social Work* 12 265-290.

Ingleby D
(1974) 'Integrating the child into a social world' in M Richards (ed) *The psychology of child psychology.* Cambridge University Press.

Jones C
(1977) 'The fate of abused children' in A W Franklin (ed) *The challenge of child abuse.* Academic Press.

Leicestershire County Council
(1980) 'Carly Taylor: report of an independent inquiry.' Leicestershire Area Health Authority.

Martin H D and Kempe C H (eds)
(1976) *The abused child.* Cambridge, Massachusetts: Ballinger Publishing Company.

Morse C W, Sahler O J Z and Friedman S B
(1970) 'A three year follow-up study of abused and neglected
children'. *American Journal of Diseases of Children* 120.

Ormrod R
(1974) 'The role of the courts in relation to children'. *Child Adoption* 75 1.

Pringle M K
(1974) *The needs of children.* Hutchinson.

Parsloe P and Stevenson O
(1978) *Social service teams: the practioner's view.* HMSO.

Polansky N A, Chalmers M A, Buttenwieser E and Williams DP
(1981) *Damaged parents: an anatomy of neglect.* Chicago: University
of Chicago Press.

Robertson J and Robertson J
(1972) 'Quality of substitute care as an influence on separation
responses'. *Journal of Psychosomatic Research* 14 4.

Royal College of Psychiatrists
(1982) 'Definitions of emotional abuse'. *Bulletin of the Royal College
of Psychiatrists* May 1982 85-87.

Rutter M and Madge N
(1976) *Cycles of disadvantage.* Heinemann.

Rutter M, Quinton D and Liddle C
(1983) 'Parenting in two generations: looking backwards and looking
forwards' in N Madge (ed) *Families at risk.* Heinemann.

Smale G
Unpublished communication with the author.

Stein T J, Gambrill E D and Wiltse K T
(1978) *Children in foster homes: achieving continuity of care.*
New York: Praeger Publications.

Wald M
(1982) 'State intervention on behalf of endangered children: a
proposed legal response.' *International Journal of Child Abuse and
Neglect* 16 1 3-45.

Wilson H
(1980) *Parental supervision – a neglect aspect of delinquency.* Stevens & Sons.

Standards of parenting and the law

Richard White

Richard White is a solicitor in private practice and was co-director of the BAAF research project on section 3 resolutions (Child Care Act 1980) under the monitoring requirements of the Children Act 1975.

Why is the law involved?

There is concern amid the increasing volume of work in child abuse and neglect that the response has been excessively legalistic. The legalism has been exhibited in two ways: expanded coercive intervention by state agencies and more frequent recourse to the law, the courts and lawyers by all parties involved with children[1].

This may in part reflect uncertainty on the part of the social work agencies and their staff about their skill in working with clients without coercive powers. Nonetheless, the law has an essential part to play in the formulation of social work aims in the child care field. Social work is about change and enabling children and their families to function appropriately. Unless we are clear what standards are 'appropriate' and that there is legislative sanction to bring about change, it may be questioned whether a social worker has any right to attempt to bring about 'change'. Even the so-called voluntary assistance inevitably has heavy overtones of coercion if the state is involved, because of its statutory responsibilities.

In summary therefore it is essential that we understand what we are trying to achieve in bringing about change and what legislative sanction there is for the action.

Legislative aims

Michael Wald has written on these issues in an American context[2]. Much of his paper is relevant to this country, so it is quoted extensively. His aim is to establish a legislative framework based on his proposals. Even though the legal system is different in the United States his proposals could form the basis of a system to operate in the United Kingdom.

In this country such legislation would not have an easy passage, both because of lack of time (and possibly lack of governmental will to legislate on such matters) and because there is little consensus about child care criteria.

Wald proposes that the legislative framework should require courts and statutory agencies to pay more attention to the welfare of children and their families, while at the same time limiting their areas of discretion. His proposals could largely be operated within our present legal system, since they establish principles which arguably form the basis for good practice.

Wald considers that there are four basic decisions to be made in any legal response to abuse and neglect:

a) What situations or harms to children justify coercive state intervention, ie how should abuse and neglect be defined for legal purposes?

b) What standards should govern the disposition of children who have been adjudicated abused or neglected, ie when should children be removed from the home of their biological parents?

c) What standards should be used in deciding when a child who has been placed in foster care should be returned to his or her biological parents?

d) What circumstances justify permanent termination of parental rights, so that the parents can never resume custody of the child?

He adds:

'Standards for termination must be related to the standards for intervention, for removing children and for returning them to their parents, in order to achieve a systematic and sensible intervention process.'

If the welfare of the child is to be promoted this is an important principle, and it is a major defect in our legislation that there is no systematic process.

Wald continues:

'Developing a system for intervention requires resolving both value and empirical questions. The decision to coercively intervene to protect a child is not solely a medical or a psychological issue; it is also a value question. We are asking what type of life each child should be guaranteed by the state, as well as the relative roles of government and family in child-rearing.'

It is important to note that we are not talking about ideal parenting (whatever that may be) but about minimal standards, ie what we may consider 'good-enough'. It is this concept of 'good-enough' parenting which has to be related to legal provisions for removal, restoration and termination.

Wald also states the importance of considering the alternative for the child if the state intervenes:

'The question of the efficacy of intervention is central to all of the proposals in this article. To a large degree, 'interventionists' and 'non-interventionists' disagree primarily on the issue of the costs and benefits, rather than on ultimate goals for children's well-being. Unfortunately, there is very little in the way of reliable data about the consequences of intervention in most cases where it currently occurs. The literature is comprised primarily of clinical studies and theoretical works about the likely impact of intervention. There is virtually no longitudinal research measuring the impact of various types of intervention.

In the absence of data, the critical point is whether one accepts the proposition that intervention can do more harm than good. This proposition seems clearest when intervention leads to removal of a child. It is now the prevailing ethic among child care experts that foster care has been over-used as a means of protecting children. Although still widely used, foster care is considered generally to be a worse alternative than leaving a child in the home.

While the data are not conclusive, the existing evidence certainly justifies a cautious policy before removing children. In the absence of much evidence as to when foster care is beneficial, limited intervention is consistent with both psychological theory and value preferences, which reflect the enormity of a decision to deprive parents of a child.'[3]

Standards for intervention and removal

Wald makes a number of important points.
'Placing a family under supervision can impair the parents' ability to provide consistent care. It is also a first step in a process that often leads to removal when the parents fail to comply with the dictates of the supervising agency. In fact, the threat of removal may be necessary to get some parents to accept services. Thus, we should only intervene when we are prepared to remove the child, if necessary.'

'Judgements about appropriate standards for coercive intervention cannot be divorced from the question of funding of the intervention system. While many experts would agree with my conclusion that current intervention efforts often are harmful to children, they might disagree with the conclusions that we should therefore favour parental autonomy and limit the discretion of judges and social workers to intervene on behalf of children. Instead, it might be argued, we should continue to intervene as frequently, or even more frequently, than at present but improve the quality of the programs offered upon intervention.'

'The standards are premised on the assumption that there will be no dramatic increase in funds available to juvenile courts and welfare departments in the near future. Given the long history of inadequate funding of these systems, there is little reason to believe that significant change will occur at this time. Therefore, it is essential to use existing resources in the most efficient way possible. This can be done best by intervening properly in the most serious cases rather than poorly in a larger number of cases.'

'Recognising the difficulty of prediction does not require ignoring the fact that the home environment has a significant effect on a child's development. A substantial body of theory and data supports the hypothesis that a child's intellectual, physical, emotional, and social development is significantly affected by his or her home environment. *However, since each child may respond differently to a given home environment, the law must focus primarily on the child rather than the parent, or home environment.'* (my emphasis)

'If our concern is with helping children who are suffering specific harms, intervention should occur whenever the parents are unwilling to rectify the situation, regardless of who caused the harm.'

'Although there may be many types of "neglectful behaviour" by parents, there are relatively few harms to children with which we should be concerned. By limiting intervention to cases in which these harms are present or are extremely likely to occur, the hazards of prediction are reduced, although not eliminated, and the law is made more efficacious. Specific laws do not prevent judges from examining each situation on its own facts in order to determine the appropriate disposition; rather they more clearly define for the judge the kinds of harm with which society is concerned.'

'Ideally parents should protect children from a large number of harms and make sure that they receive a variety of benefits. Obviously parents should be required to feed and clothe their children. They also must comply with laws regarding compulsory education and child labour. Beyond these minimums, parents should provide love, affection, and a home environment conducive to the development of mental and emotional stability in their children. Ideally each home would provide each child the opportunity to fulfil his or her potential in society.'

'Probably few families provide this "ideal" environment. Yet in a system based on parental autonomy, the fact that parents are less than perfect should not justify intervention. In the light of our limited knowledge and the limited alternatives to raising children in their 'natural' families, coercive intervention should be statutorily authorised only if (1) the harm is serious; and (2) it is a type of harm for which, in general, the remedy of coercive intervention will do more good than harm.'

'These criteria reflect the judgement that certain categories of harm to children should not constitute a statutory basis for intervention, even though in some individual cases intervention will do more good than harm. The criteria are intended to ensure that "state" views of child rearing will replace parental views only when the threatened harm is of a magnitude that justifies the risks and costs of intervention. In addition, limiting intervention to the classes of harms that are most serious helps ensure that the limited resources available for helping children will go to helping those in the most danger. Intervention should be concentrated where the risks of non-intervention are greatest.'

The conclusion is inescapable; that ideally 'good-enough' parenting must be defined in relation to the individual child, and that accordingly standards should be drawn in relation to the harm or benefit to the child.

Statutory grounds for intervention
(The detail of Wald's proposals is not necessarily approved, but they demonstrate how more definite criteria must be established. In particular it is doubted whether they provide adequately for the child who is *frequently* subject to more minor neglect or abuse.'[4])

The standards which Wald proposes are as follows:

In cases where it is alleged that a child is endangered, courts should be authorised to assume court jurisdiction in order to continue parental custody upon the parents accepting supervision or to remove a child from his or her home, only if the court finds that the child comes within one or more of the provisions in subsections (a) to (f).
a) A child has suffered a physical injury, inflicted non-accidentally, causing death, disfigurement, impairment of body functioning, or severe bodily harm, or there is a substantial likelihood that the child imminently will suffer such an injury.

b) A child has suffered physical injury causing death, disfigurement, impairment of body functioning, or severe bodily harm as a result of conditions uncorrected by his or her parents or by the failure of his or her parents to supervise adequately or protect the child; or there is a substantial risk that the child imminently will suffer such harms as a result of conditions uncorrected by his or her parents or by the failure of his or her parents to adequately supervise or protect the child.

c) A child is suffering serious emotional damage, evidenced by severe anxiety, depression or withdrawal, or untoward aggressive behaviour towards others, and his or her parents are unwilling to provide, when financially able to do so, or to permit, necessary treatment.

d) A child has been sexually abused by a member of his or her household.

e) A child is in need of medical treatment to cure, alleviate, or prevent serious physical harm that may cause death, disfigurement, or substantial impairment of bodily functioning, and his or her parents are unwilling to provide, when financially able to do so, or consent to, the medical treatment.

f) A child is committing delinquent acts as a result of parental encouragement, guidance or approval.

Dispositions
a) *General standard:* The goal of all dispositions should be to protect the child from the harm justifying intervention.

b) *Dispositions other than removal of the child:* In ordering a disposition other than removal of the child from his or her home, the court should choose a program designed to alleviate the immediate danger to the child, to mitigate or cure any damage the child has already suffered, and to aid the parents so that the child will not be endangered in the future. In selecting a program, the court should choose those services that least interfere with family autonomy, provided that the services are adequate to protect the child.

c) *Removal:* A child should not be removed from his or her home and placed in foster care unless the court finds that:
    The child has been physically abused as defined in Section (a) above and there is a *preponderance of evidence*[5] that the child cannot be protected from further physical abuse without being removed; or
    The child has been endangered in one of the other ways specified in Section (a) above and there is *clear and convincing* evidence that the child cannot be protected from further harm of the type justifying intervention unless removed from his or her home.

Regardless of whether any child is removed from his or her home, the court must find that there is a placement available in which the child will not be endangered.

How far can Wald's principles be implemented within the English legal system?

The legislative provisions in England and Wales

The provisions with which we are concerned are contained in the Children and Young Persons Act 1969, the Child Care Act 1980, the Children Act 1975, the Matrimonial Causes Act 1973, the Guardianship Acts 1971 and 1973, and within the wardship jurisdiction.

Children and Young Persons Act 1969
By S.1(2) a juvenile court may make an order (usually a care or supervision order) in respect of a child if satisfied (inter alia) that:
'his proper development is being avoidably prevented or neglected or his health is being avoidably impaired or neglected or he is being ill-treated'
and that
'the child is in need of care or control which he is unlikely to receive unless the court makes an order'

There is little guidance as to the meaning of these provisions, but it is commonly held that they require circumstances to have occurred which will have caused some disadvantage to the child, and that magistrates may not predict that some disadvantage will occur. The degree of disadvantage required is a matter for the discretion of the court, and even if some disadvantage is proved to exist the court is not required to make an order. It should be noted that the Act provides for an objective assessment of development. What remains unanswered is what development is 'proper'. Presumably if parenting was 'good-enough' then equally the development would be satisfactory. The need for care or control means that the court can only be satisfied if the order would achieve some improvement in care or control.

This Act satisfies some of Wald's criteria in that it focuses on the child and enables the court to make a finding without necessitating removal of the child. As it stands it is not specific enough, but it does *permit* a court to operate strict standards. Nonetheless, the Act provides very wide discretion to courts and local authorities in the exercise of their powers.

Child Care Act 1980
Apparently stricter are the provisions under the 1980 Act which empower a local authority to assume parental rights in respect of a

child in 'voluntary care'. However, in practice they are equally vague since they rely on concepts like the parent is 'incapable or unfit' to care for the child. Additionally, the transfer of rights should be 'in the interests' of the child, but it is not necessary to specify what harm might befall the child if the rights are not transferred from parent to state.

This Act does not satisfy Wald's standards because it focuses on parental behaviour rather than harm to the child, though it relates of course to cases where the child is already separated from the parents. In such cases the standards proposed for return or termination should be applied as they are set out subsequently.

Welfare provisions
Recently children have been committed to the care of local authorities under the terms of provisions in the Children Act 1975, the Matrimonial Causes Act 1973, the Guardianship Acts 1971 and 1973, and in wardship proceedings. All these Acts are similar in that the court may commit to care if 'there are exceptional circumstances making it impracticable or undesirable for the child to be under the care of either of his parents...' However, decisions under these Acts must also take into account the general requirement in S.1 of the Guardianship of Minors Act 1971, that 'Where in any proceedings before any court...the legal custody or upbringing of a minor...is in question, the court...shall regard the welfare of the minor as the first and paramount consideration'. These provisions are the most unspecific.

With all the statutes, wide discretion is left to the agencies to decide on the arguments they will put before the court and on the court to decide what it thinks is in the interests of the child. This has the disadvantage that many parents may, and do, not know what is required of them, but it does enable agencies to establish their own standards, make them clear to parents, negotiate with parents over them and argue their standards and the application of them in court subsequently if necessary. Thus Wald's standards for removal could be practised within our system.

Work before separation

Would the standards proposed enable a local authority to provide social work assistance at an early enough stage? Standards have to be related to circumstances in which the child could be removed, if services are provided by court order. If services are accepted on a voluntary basis, working within the proposed legal framework offers two options. Services can be intended to improve a marginal situation without the intention of removal if they are unsuccessful. Alternatively, services can be offered where the child would otherwise be removed. In either case the purpose and possible outcomes of social work involvement should be made clear.

After separation

Practice in England has tended to concentrate on short-term decisions surrounding removal and insufficiently about placement. Except in the High Court, the court has no say about placement[6], and discretion is left entirely with the local authority.

Wald's standards create a framework for providing the child with 'good-enough' parenting after removal. He says:

'It is now widely acknowledged that the system of care when children are removed is less than ideal. The foremost problem is the instability of foster care – the failure to provide stable homes for children. Thus this section proposes standards for the two alternative post-placement dispositions – returning the child to the natural parents or termination of parental rights and permanent placement in a new home. The central premise of the proposals is that one of these alternatives must be selected within a specific time after placement in order to ensure that placement is a temporary interlude in the child's life.'

In reaching decisions and establishing standards for post-separation issues Wald suggests four questions should be considered:

'First, how likely is it that a child who has to be removed under the standards previously proposed will ever be returned to his or her parents? Put another way, are there many instances where a child can be protected from further harm only by removal, yet after removal conditions in his or her home would improve sufficiently so that he or she could be returned home without being endangered again?

Second, what harms to a child are likely to result from:
● being removed from home, placed in a temporary living situation for any given period of time, and then returned home
● being removed, placed in temporary care, and ultimately never returned home – in this regard we need to consider instances where the child is put in multiple placements and instances where this is a single placement
● having parental rights terminated, either immediately or at some time after removal

Third, how many parents will be harmed or benefited by any given standards?

Fourth, what are the consequences of adopting any set of standards on the workings of the entire placement system?'

He concludes:

'While not providing conclusive answers to the questions posed at the beginning of this section, the best available theory and data do indicate that subjecting children to lengthy foster care, especially if this involves multiple placements, causes both short and long-run serious harm to the child. Moreover, it seems clear that the longer the child is in placement the less likely he or she is to be returned home or provided with another permanent home.

However, the data do not support claims that short, temporary placement, followed by return to the natural parents or placement in a new stable environment, seriously damages most children. Children appear to be able to maintain two or more attachments, develop new attachments, if not subjected to repeated separations. Moreover, the data indicate that precipitous termination might destroy important parent-child bonds and not result in providing a new, permanent placement.

Therefore, I reject a policy permitting immediate termination upon removal, absent compelling evidence that reunion is unlikely or re-injury likely. Instead, the proposed standards adopt the current premise that removal is for a temporary period with the goal being to return the child as quickly as possible. The next section contains proposals designed to minimise the trauma of separation and to facilitate rapid return. However, return will often be impossible. The following section proposes a new legal standard for termination of parental rights, designed to move children out of temporary placements before they are harmed thereby and before they are locked into permanent foster care'.

Experience suggests that if these standards are adopted, and we do identify more specifically circumstances in which intervention is undertaken, there will need to be changes. Wald says:

'If we are to adopt a system that is committed to returning children as quickly as possible, many changes in present practice will be needed. In many jurisdictions court and agency policies and practices ignore the goal of returning the child; in some jurisdictions the policies actually serve to defeat this goal.

There has been a great deal written on the need for, and ways of achieving, a permanent planning process, designed to eliminate long-term, unstable foster care. It must be recognised, however, that while many agencies and courts have a permanent planning system, very few institutions have established a working, complete planning process. The permanent planning requires significant systemic change, with entirely different attitudes as well as practices.'

A court review system may ultimately be necessary to enforce change. Wald's arguments are:

'Clearly internal agency review does not provide an adequate check: court hearings provide a forum in which the parents and the child, through his or her attorney, can challenge any agency's inaction. A court review is superior to lodging a complaint with the agency, since parents likely will assume that the high authorities within the agency will support the caseworker. Moreover, the presence of counsel at a court hearing may make it easier for parents to raise complaints about the agency.

In addition, court hearings provide a mechanism for reviewing parental performance so that it can be determined whether they have shown an interest in resuming custody. At each hearing both the supervising agency and the child's attorney can document the parent's failure, if any, to work toward resuming custody. It is essential that parental non-cooperation be documented as soon as possible, otherwise it will be difficult to obtain termination when necessary. In a number of cases, courts have refused to order termination because the judge sympathised with the claim that the agency had not provided services, had discouraged visitation, or had made return difficult. Courts hearing termination cases will be less concerned about such problems if there have been prior court reviews.

Third, a court review may serve as an incentive to both the agency and the parents. Social workers will attempt to conform their behaviour to the court's expectations in order to avoid criticism at review hearings. The realisation that the court will review their conduct, and possibly terminate parental rights, may induce parents to show greater interest in their children.'

The court would make factual findings to provide a basis for local authority practice. Such findings might cover:
1. what services have been offered and provided to the parents to facilitate reunion

2. whether the parents are satisfied with the services

3. the extent to which the parents have visited the child and any reasons why visitation has not occurred or has been infrequent

4. whether the agency is satisfied with the co-operation received from the parents

5. whether additional services are needed to facilitate the return of the minor to his or her parents

6. when the return of the child can be expected

Return of the child to the parents

These considerations lead to the standard for returning the child to his parents:

> 'A child should be returned home at the review hearing unless the court finds by a preponderance of the evidence that the child will be endangered in the manner specified in Sections (a)–(f) above if returned home or that return would be seriously detrimental to the physical or emotional well-being of the child.'[7]

This is clearly a contentious matter and would represent a clear change in policy and practice in this country, but it is important if we are to establish more specific standards than exist at present.

Wald admits:

> 'Some children will be returned who are thriving in foster care. Even though their well-being may deteriorate at home, that cost is outweighed by the benefit of making foster care truly temporary. As a result, the best decision, from each child's perspective, cannot be made in every case. The best is that which promotes the best interests of most children.'

He goes on, illustrating the difficulties of establishing that the parents should be entitled to have the child back, to consider a vital question of this debate.

> 'The burden of proof question is critical in the return decision process. Because the substantive standard requires a prediction about the likelihood of future endangerment, conclusive evidence cannot be produced by either the parents seeking return or the agency opposing it. Given the difficulty of making such predictions with a high degree of certainty, placement of the burden will be determinative in many cases.
>
> A substantial case can be made for placing the burden on the parents. It would be a safe course from the standpoint of protecting the child from re-injury since fewer returns would occur and fewer risks would be taken. In addition, placing the burden on parents may encourage them to make stronger efforts to resume custody. Finally, it is the parents who are seeking to change the status quo and, in general, the law places the burden on this party.
>
> Despite these considerations, I propose putting the burden on the agency. First, although conclusive proof of future harm is

unavailable to both sides, to the extent that implications about future harm can be raised, the agency clearly has greater access to pertinent information and the greater ability to persuade the court. For example, the agency can show that the parents have not co-operated with a treatment program, have not shown an interest in the child, or have failed to care for other children in the home. It can also produce expert testimony indicating that because of a mental condition, alcoholism or some other problem, the parents probably will endanger the child again. Given such evidence, a judge is unlikely to return the child.

While the parents cannot prove that the home environment will be safe until they have resumed custody, the agency can test the safety of the home environment by returning the child home on a gradual basis, starting with one-day visits and progressing to visits of several days, before a final decision is made. The caseworker can observe the parent-child interaction during these visits to determine whether the child can be protected. Of course, parents will act differently under such conditions, but such procedures should uncover homes that remain clearly dangerous.

Second, placing the burden on the parents may prolong foster care for many children. Since the parents rarely would be able to prove the home safe, judges would probably take the conservative course and leave the child in care until the agency recommends return. I prefer striking the balance between the risk of re-injury and the risk of lengthy foster care in favour of allowing the parents to regain custody of their children.

This problem would not arise under the termination standards I propose since termination would occur, in most cases, within a year of removal if the child cannot be returned. However, if these termination standards are adopted a separate justification for placing the burden on the agency arises. Under the proposed system, if the child is not returned termination generally will follow. Increasing the number of terminations is essential if children are to be provided with stable, continuous living environments. Yet before resorting to termination, a substantial drastic step from the parents' perspective, the state should be required to prove that the child cannot be returned to his or her parents.'

These arguments demonstrate the importance of the local authority operating on clearly established criteria on the lines of the other papers in this publication and presenting a carefully prepared case to the court.

Grounds for termination

As was argued at the beginning of the paper, the whole question of standards relies on a proper relationship between removal, restoration and termination. In order to provide continuity and consistency throughout the care system termination standards must follow from removal and failure to restore.

Wald's principles are:

'1. *Termination after a child is in placement*
a) If a child is removed without termination of parental rights, the court must consider the need for termination at the twelve month review hearing if the child cannot be returned home at the time.
   i For children who were under three at the time of placement, termination should be ordered at this point unless the court finds by clear and convincing evidence that an exception specified in Section 2 below applies.
   ii For children over three at the time of placement, termination should not be ordered at this point, unless the court finds that the parents have failed to maintain contact with the child during the previous six months and to reasonably plan for resumption of care of the child. The court should not order termination if one of the exceptions specified in Section 2 below applies.'

Wald now believes that children under two require special consideration if they have been seriously abused. He suggests that parents who abuse such children are disturbed and different from abusers of older children. The court should be required to consider early termination in the light of the harm to the child, the circumstances leading to the injury and the emotional condition of the parents. [8]

'b) When a child over three at the time of initial removal remains in care for eighteen months termination shall be ordered unless one of the exceptions applies.

2. *Situations in which termination should not be ordered*
When a child would otherwise come within the provision of Section 1 above, a court should not order termination if it finds by clear and convincing evidence that any of the following are applicable:
a) Because of the closeness of the parent-child relationship, it would be seriously detrimental to the child to terminate parental rights at this time.

b) Because of the nature of the child's problems, the child is placed in a residential treatment facility, and continuation of parental rights will not prevent finding the child a permanent family placement if the parents cannot resume custody when residential care is no longer needed.

c) The child is placed with a relative who does not want to adopt the child.

d) The child cannot or should not be placed permanently in a family environment. If the child cannot presently be placed in a permanent family environment, the court must also find the failure to terminate will not impair the child's opportunity for a permanent placement in a family setting.'

These standards may be considered severe for parents, especially if they have suffered as a result of social and economic inequalities, as well as from discriminatory practices in the delivery of social services. Wald defends this by saying:

'The system proposed in this article attempts to minimise such discrimination by making the grounds for intervention as culturally unbiased as possible, by limiting the discretion of decision makers, by requiring maximum efforts to keep families together before removal and maximum efforts to reunite families after removal, and by providing counsel and other procedural safeguards to the parents and child.

Still, discrimination may continue. I choose not to make children suffer additionally in order to rectify the injustices to their parents. We can at least protect the children, even if society will not treat their parents fairly.'

Conclusion

In view of the inconsistent attitude of the courts in the last few years, it may be considered doubtful whether they would at the present time support the standards, but there is more likelihood that they would if children came into care less frequently and after maximum efforts to keep families together and reunite them after removal. The current provisions for making a child free for adoption under S.14 of the Children Act 1975, which are closest to the Wald proposals for termination, are rather more vague. They require the court to exercise discretion in relation to the welfare of the child and, if the parent does not agree to the order, to consider whether there are grounds for dispensing with agreement.

The approach proposed accords with the permanence philosophy of only permitting removal of the child when it is essential, of permitting periods in care for as short a time as possible, and of providing a permanent home for the child by reinforcement of the child's family of origin or by an alternative long-term placement. The provisions reflect the importance of considering carefully why the child should remain in care long-term, if that is the plan, rather than be placed with people who will take full legal responsibility for them.

One important question, which the standards do not appear to address adequately, concerns children with frequent minor injuries or received into care on numerous occasions for short periods. Can we say how many times we permit recurrence of injuries, neglect or disinterest, before terminating parental rights?

In reaching decisions and presenting cases to the courts it is important to try and establish some basis on which to judge the welfare of the child. Concepts like ill-treatment, neglect and abandonment and proper development provide some guidance but do not adequately reflect concerns about the parenting of children. A central question for the law is whether it is possible and/or desirable to be more specific about statutory provisions perhaps in terms of harm to the child. The alternative is that the judiciary and statutory agencies superimpose their own interpretation depending on their own views, current customs and sometimes the evidence they hear from professional witnesses.

Notes

1. One effect of this has been the increased use of wardship in the last decade. Applications have increased from 1203 in 1975 to 2301 in 1982. (Judicial Statistics)

2. See *International journal of child abuse and neglect* for full text, 1982 16 1 3-45.

3. The work of Lynch and Roberts *(Consequences of child abuse* Academic Press, 1982.) now demonstrates the harm that can be done through abuse. Since his article Wald has commented that recent research indicates that foster care can provide benefits, but that we still know too little about it (private correspondence).

4. Wald accepts this point but comments that it is the focus on the child which is important. If removal is thought to be necessary where there are frequent minor injuries, perhaps the conditions in (b) or (c) should still be required.

5. The English standard is 'the balance of probabilities'.

6. The County Court has power to make directions under the Matrimonial Causes Act 1973, but rarely exercises the power.

7. Since the article was written, a new preferred standard for return has been incorporated in the California code:
> 'A child must be returned unless the court finds that return will create a substantial risk of serious detriment to the child's physical or emotional well-being.'

This places marginally less emphasis on return, but still requires the authority to justify retaining the child in care. The change in criteria does not affect the arguments in the rest of the section.

8. Views expressed in private correspondence. This type of case is decreasing in frequency in the United Kingdom. See S. Creighton, *Trends in child abuse,* NSPCC, 1984.

Parenting and parenting failure: some guidelines for the assessment of the child, his parents and the family

Dr Arnon Bentovim and Liza Bingley

Dr Arnon Bentovim is Consultant Psychiatrist and Liza Bingley is Research Fellow at the Department of Psychological Medicine, The Hospital for Sick Children, Great Ormond Street.

As helping professionals, the issue of assessing parenting and parenting failure arises in the context of practice rather than as an abstract phenomenon. The need to assess parenting arises when a child's physical and/or psychological state begs the question as to the causative links between the child's problems and the parenting he has received. Such problems include:

- child abuse – eg, suspected physical abuse, such as unexplained injuries, fractures, bruising and poisoning, all of which can be life-threatening
- neglect, failure to thrive syndromes and growth failure
- suspected emotional abuse, whether through active rejection or accommodation to distorted family demands, expectations and situations
- suspected sexual abuse
- when planning is necessary for a child's future – eg, consideration of rehabilitation, fostering and adoption where there has been abandonment, rejection or family breakdown.

To recognise the presence of parenting failure we first have to establish some of the key expectations that society has of parents. For a child's potential to unfold, parents need to provide an environment in which the child can grow adequately in an atmosphere of security, affection and acceptance; be protected from danger and be nurtured and controlled adequately. The child also needs to be able to play and have sufficient freedom to explore and to learn; parents are also expected to ensure children are educated and attention paid to medical needs.

Therefore, in the event of parenting failure being suspected, these functions should be evaluated in order to assess how well the child's needs are being met. We find there are certain key questions which need to be considered:

- How do presenting problems in the child relate to their context in terms of the present family circumstances, the past experiences of

the family and the nature of the involvement of the professional network already involved with the family?
- What changes are necessary to ensure that the child's problem can be reversed? These changes may need to be in the parenting, the child and/or the resources made available from outside the family.
- What are the possibilities for change in the parents, the child and the family's social environment, including the extended family and the professional network? This may entail an assessment of whether alternative parenting is necessary, including an evaluation of the benefits and dangers involved, and the potential responses of the child and family.

In order to begin to answer some of these questions we need a number of frameworks into which to fit our observations and information about the family.

Aids to assist in the assessment of parenting and parenting failure

Observations of the child

Standardised observations of the child and of changes in the child's behaviour and emotional responses over time are central to an assessment of the current state of parenting. The parenting required by different children varies according to their particular needs and may be highly specific, for example in the case of a severely handicapped child. For instance, Jean 'A', a girl of six months, who was the subject of a number of case conferences, had first come to the notice of professionals through the low frequency of parental visiting, and her parents' poor handling of her in hospital following treatment for a renal condition. Her mother had grown up in care, was living in temporary accommodation, and had never worked. She was socially isolated and only had a very tenuous link with a boyfriend. It was then realised by the medical staff that Jean was blind, at which point the professionals involved were forced to raise their expectations of Jean's mother if she was to be able to take on the full-time care of her child. For under these circumstances there was a real risk that Jean's language and social skills would not develop to their full potential without considerable input and stimulation from her caretaker. Therefore the professionals involved had to set as criteria a far more intensive programme of visiting and willingness to learn new skills on the part of Jean's mother than would have been the case for a normal child.

It is important that we have a variety of means of being able to observe detailed developmental changes in children over time. These include the use of:
- sequential measures of height, weight and head circumference
- child development schemata as described, for example, by

46

Fahlberg (1981) covering a number of developmental areas and the state of attachments to significant figures
- longitudinal cognitive testing including the assessment of speech, language and play
- regular observation of the child's performance in school or nursery
- regular observation of the emotional status of the child

Observation of parenting and of family functioning
Despite our awareness that the needs and development of children are closely inter-linked with the development of parenting skills and qualities, we do need to look at these factors separately. We will examine the following frameworks for the assessment of parenting:
- the 'level of living' provided for the child
- present family functioning
- the significance of family history.

The 'childhood level of living scale'
Polansky in his recent book, *Damaged parents — an anatomy of neglect* (1981), has made a major contribution to the subject of assessing parenting with his 'childhood level of living scale'. The scale was originally developed as an aid to assessing the adequacy of child care in urban settings and is essentially an extensive questionnaire to be completed by the professional about the child and his predicament. The areas covered in the scale provide the professional with a useful focus for the assessment of both the actual development of the child and, in a very concrete way, the standard of care in the child's living setting. Because the family's position on the scale is not permanent, the scale aids the professional in defining more precisely what changes need to take place, both within the family and in terms of the provision of material resources, in order to improve the child's level of living.

The scale is divided into two basic areas — one is concerned with physical care and other with the stimulation and the emotional care of the child. (See page 108)

The 'childhood level of living scale' is used to produce an overall score which can be matched against Polansky's examples of severely neglectful parents. We would argue that it could be used by professionals as a check list to help look at areas of parenting in detail.

The assessment of family functioning
Although consideration of the parent/child relationship is essential to an assessment of parenting, parenting is only one facet of the multi-faceted system which is the family. The child's problem must therefore be seen in the light of other family ingredients such as the

marital relationship, the relationship with the extended family, sibling relationships and the parents' previous experiences as children and adults. Such factors combine together in a bewildering fashion but we consider that there are certain basic tasks that the family has to perform. A central task is that children are nurtured and yet able to grow away from the family. This means that there needs to be a balance within the family between factors which foster stability – ie, sameness and attachment – and factors which promote adaptability and growth – ie, difference, change and separation. In families where children are manifesting problems related to parenting failure, we often find forces within the family which maintain and lock individuals into dysfunctional patterns of parental care and child response. These patterns, if seen in the whole family context, may be open to change by means of therapeutic intervention. If it is possible to define the areas in which the family as a system is in difficulty, then we can begin to delineate the changes that have to occur if the child's development is to be facilitated.

At The Hospital for Sick Children we have developed three approaches to assessing families which we have found useful:
- *the summary format of family functioning (SFFF)*, which is a guide to the systematic description of family functioning
- *the family health scales (FHS)*, which provide a global assessment of family functioning
- *a focal assessment of the family*, which links the presenting problem in the child, the presenting family circumstances and the past experiences of both the parents and the children.

The SFFF and FHS both look at the key areas of family competence which should be considered when assessing how a family functions. The summary format of family functioning provides a written and detailed description of these areas of family functioning. The family health scales allow the measurement of the overall functioning of families along a continuum of family functioning ranging from breakdown of functioning through clear dysfunction and adequate functioning, to optimal functioning.

The concept of family functioning used in both the SFFF and the FHS is based on the premise that the family in our society is expected to:
- provide for the physical and emotional nurturance of both adults and children
- ensure the socialisation of the children
- foster and maintain the emotional health and stability of all family members.

These primary responsibilities and duties represent a combination of the needs of individual members and the expectations of society.

They are, of course, shared with people and institutions other than the family such as relatives, neighbours, friends, schools and the health and social services. Effective family functioning is the carrying out of these broad responsibilities and duties, which may, themselves, be broken down into more specific family tasks, such as getting the children to school and looking after sick family members. The carrying out of these tasks requires that family members interact with one another in a co-ordinated and constructive manner. Thus, the effectiveness of family functioning can be linked with the quality of family interaction.

In the assessment of family functioning, we consider seven main dimensions of family interaction:

- *Affective status* which refers to the emotional life of the family including family atmosphere and the nature and quality of the relationships within the family. In a family at the point of breakdown in functioning, for example, family atmosphere may be dead, panicky or chaotic and the relationships may be perverse, attacking, devaluing or grossly over-dependent.
- *Communication* which looks at the verbal and non-verbal interchange between family members, including the expression and reception of messages. Communication breakdown in a family can severely affect their functioning if, for instance, family members have chaotic, fragmented or disrupted patterns of communicating with one another, or if they are unable to talk or listen to each other.
- *Boundaries* which determine the degree of separateness and connectedness between family members, with family cohesion, inter-generational boundaries and individual autonomy being the main constituents. Individual autonomy and development are likely to be seriously impaired if some or all of the members are grossly over-involved, or largely isolated from one another. Excessively rigid or blurred inter-generational boundaries, in particular, are likely to make it very difficult for a family to carry out its primary responsibilities.
- *Alliances* which looks at the pattern of relationships within the family and at the nature and quality of specific relationships including the parental and the parent/child relationship. The pattern of alliances in a family may contain serious deficiencies such as marked splits, scapegoating or triangling, or the isolation of all family members, and this may make the parental coalition, for instance, unworkable.
- *Stability* which refers to the sense of continuity of a family unit, and *Adaptability* which is linked to the family's capacity to respond to changing demands and circumstances. When assessing a family at the point of breakdown, the family stability may be precarious, with the family having a sense of imminent break-up, or being maintained at the cost of severe and pervasive patho-

logical family interaction. Roles and relationships may be fixed, rigid or chaotic making it impossible for the family to adapt to changing needs or circumstances.

- *Family competence* which relates to operations such as conflict resolution, decision making, problem solving and the management of the children's behaviour. The competence of the family in these areas is central to resolving family difficulties. If, for example, conflicts are ignored, displaced or dominate family life, or if the family cannot recognise problems or tackle them, their level of functioning is likely to be low. Families in which the parents have markedly inappropriate or confusing expectations of their children, or whose control of the children's behaviour is absent, chaotic or rigid may well have reached a point of breakdown in their functioning.

- *Relationship to the environment* which looks at the family's capacity to make links with the outside world. A family which is cut off, insular or threatened by contact with the outside world, or alternatively, which has no distinct family identity, is likely to have serious problems in resolving family difficulties. This may include the family being unable to make use of professional and other resources available to them in the community.

Problems of parenting failure can therefore be more fully understood if they are placed in the context of an assessment of the whole family looking at these specific aspects of family functioning.

Focal assessment of the family
Once we have obtained some measure of the child's state and an assessment of the family functioning, we need to have some way of linking these together with the history of the family and the individuals within it. In a series of publications (Kinston and Bentovim, etc.), we have developed the concept of the family focus as a way of organising or coherently bringing together the complex and extensive data which is gathered when assessing families. Using the notion of the family focus, it becomes possible to reduce this information to a usable formulation which can explain the presenting problem in the child, both in the context of the way that the family is functioning in the here and now, and also in the context of the family's history. It has now become widely accepted that a variety of forms of abuse are seen as the culmination of a series of events over time, and these may include events in the lives of the adults as children and in the children's lives. Our observations seem to indicate that, in order to understand the ways problems in a child have arisen, it is extremely important to know what particular major stressful events have occurred in the families of origin and the current family. It is also relevant to know what meaning these events have for the current family. Thus we note that some families appear to have to constantly recreate the problems that one or both parents

experienced and struggled with as children, whilst other families seem to deny or delete significant past experiences. Still other families seem to have to seek an outsider or a scapegoat to blame for family difficulties. Alternatively, parents may seek to make up for their own past traumas or deprivations in the way they treat and handle their own children.

In order to make a focus of this sort of family information, we need to link up our observation of the problem and the typical or characteristic patterns of interaction of the family. These have then to be understood in the light of past events in the family's history which still seem to persist and remain unresolved.

This can guide the professional in defining what needs to change in the family's understanding of the problem and give him some idea of how he would recognise such change in terms of family behaviour.

Case example

Presenting problem
Joanne was brought at the age of seven months for an assessment of whether it was possible for her to be rehabilitated with her parents. She had been in care with foster parents since an injury which she sustained at the age of four weeks. At that time she had been brought to the hospital by her parents with pain and loss of movement in one leg. This was diagnosed as a fractured femur, and the injury had occurred whilst her mother, Sarah, was out shopping. Her father, David, told the police that he had been asleep with Joanne on his lap and that she had fallen off. This account was not accepted, so a place of safety order was taken, and David was prosecuted for causing grievous bodily harm. By this time, he had admitted to the police that he had been rough with Joanne when changing her nappy, and said he was anxious because he thought Sarah, Joanne's mother, had stolen his giro cheque.

Joanne was placed with short-term foster parents soon after, and a series of interim care orders were made. A decision now had to be made as to whether Joanne could be safely rehabilitated with her parents, or whether she needed an alternative family.

Observations of the child
Joanne was described by her experienced foster mother as being an anxious baby, who needed patient and sensitive handling. By the time of the assessment, having been in the placement for three months, Joanne had become attached to her foster mother. She also responded well to her parents provided they were calm and consistent in their handling of her. When they were tense or depressed and held her poorly, however, she became rigid, extremely alert and cried inconsolably, so much so that several observers felt

she might have some degree of spasticity. There was, however, no evidence of neurological damage, and her development was age-appropriate in all respects, due in part to the excellent care-taking she had received from her foster mother. To continue to thrive, therefore, Joanne was likely to need handling that was consistently calm, and responsive to her cues. Otherwise, her sensitivity might result in her crying with considerable intensity, therefore making her vulnerable to re-abuse.

Childhood level of living

Physical care

At the time of Joanne's birth, her mother, Sarah, was in a depressed and withdrawn state as a result of the death of her four year-old son, Andrew, five months before Joanne was born. Andrew was the product of a previous partnership. Sarah also had phlebitis and a pulmonary embolism at the time of Joanne's premature birth. She was physically unable to care for Joanne on discharge from hospital, so David had to look after both mother and baby.

In material terms, David had been unemployed for a year and the family had run up large rent and fuel bills. They lived in poor quality council accommodation, following a series of moves due to the parents having separated several times before the accident which caused Andrew's death. Although the couple had had constant budgeting problems, there had been no signs of negligence in their physical care of Andrew or their house. Whilst Joanne was in care, they had kept the house compulsively clean. The one exception to this pattern had been at the time of Andrew's accident. He and his mother had been travelling on a bus, and were about to dismount. The doors were opened by the driver prior to the bus stopping and mother had allowed Andrew to hold on to the handle by the door on his own. Andrew had obeyed his mother's rule, only to let go when the doors opened and had fallen out of the bus and been killed instantly. The driver of the bus is to be prosecuted for negligence.

Emotional and cognitive care

There had been no criticism of Sarah's emotional care of Andrew, nor of the stimulation she provided. Because Andrew and his mother had been together alone for a considerable time, Andrew had taken on a somewhat parental role, and Sarah was very attentive to him.

Although Sarah and David had visited Joanne regularly while she was with her foster mother, they were only just beginning to experience their separation and distance from Joanne, and to want her back. It was therefore clear that this attachment to her was only now starting to develop. The foster mother had noticed that David had always been more tuned in to Joanne's emotional cues than Sarah, but by the time of the assessment interview, Sarah was also beginning to make eye-contact with Joanne, to play with her and to cuddle her. At this stage, both parents found it difficult to handle Joanne when she was distressed and were glad to hand her back to her foster mother when she was in this state.

Family functioning
In this case, as Joanne was living with a foster family, we were interested in assessing not only the relationships in Joanne's natural family, but also those in her foster family and between her parents and her foster parents as well as the other professionals working with the family.

Affective status
It was clear that there had been an atmosphere of resentment and suspicion between the parents, Sarah and David, resulting from earlier marital difficulties and separations, as well as Andrew's death, which had occurred whilst David was away from the family, and Joanne's physical abuse. In the assessment, there was evidence of mutual blaming continuing, though this was interspersed with more supportive comments. The couple were just emerging from their sense of numbness over the loss of Andrew, and were beginning to grieve openly for him, as well as for Joanne's absence. Joanne was responsive to her parents and became tense and distressed when they were upset. There was a warm, supportive relationship between the foster mother and the parents. The social worker, too, was sympathetic and responsive to Sarah and David and they appeared to trust him, even though he had only taken over their case recently. The interviewers found themselves responding sympathetically both to the parents' pain and the efforts they were making to face the grief they felt.

Communication
Communication between Joanne's parents was stilted and uncomfort-able, but they were clearly making efforts to overcome what, by their own description, had been a major difficulty of communication between them. In the past, they had been unable to express their feelings or wishes to one another, and there had been a pattern of long periods of silence followed by emotional outbursts and violence which led to the couple separating temporarily.

The parents were able to listen to the foster mother's observations, and she, in turn, could respond sympathetically and appropriately to their discomfort at someone else caring for their child. The social worker, too, was positive and warm towards the parents, though inevitably they were suspicious and unsure of him, his seniors and previous workers, fearing that they might want to keep Joanne away from them.

Boundaries

The couple presented as more cohesive than they had evidently been previously, although they had had a period of isolation from one another, and there were still periods when Sarah was cut off when she was thinking about Andrew. This, in turn, activated considerable distress on Joanne's part, to such an extent that she became inaccessible to David so that he could not comfort her.

The foster mother's appropriate responsiveness to Joanne enabled her to deal with the baby's distress. Both the foster mother and the social worker maintained a relationship with the parents which was neither distant, rigid and critical nor over-identified, intrusive or over-sympathetic.

Alliances

At the time of the assessment, the parents were obviously closer to each other than previously. They described the time when the abusive incident occurred as having been a period of marked splits, mutual distrust and hostility between them with Joanne being scapegoated or treated roughly by father as part of an indirect attack on Sarah.

The parents could acknowledge each other's strengths and difficulties in handling Joanne, and their coalition in sharing the care of Joanne seemed workable. The relationship between the foster mother and the parents and social worker was also mutually supportive.

Stability and adaptability

The family had obviously been through a considerable period of instability, parental separation and disaster – including the death of Andrew and Joanne's abuse and the events surrounding it. It appeared that in the face of the care proceedings, the fostering and the social work help being offered had very much challenged Sarah and David's capacity to parent and that they were now beginning to show that they could respond to the demands being made on them. Sarah had, of her own volition, referred herself to a therapeutic community locally, and she and David seemed prepared to visit Joanne intensively in order to improve their relationship with her. Their awareness and sharing of their various losses had served to bring them closer together, but it remained to be seen how far this would persist over a trial period of rehabilitation with Joanne.

Family competence

Although there was some evidence of incompetence over financial management and also of Sarah's tendency, in the past, to recourse to drug-taking and forgery, the physical care of the children as such had never been seriously questioned until now. Sarah's compulsive cleaning reflected some of the energy available for caretaking. During calm periods both parents responded skillfully to Joanne and engaged in age-appropriate play with her, indicating their ability to relate to her. Under stress both parents became less competent in their handling of Joanne. Sarah and David did seem to be able to sustain some discussion about the painful issues that had divided them as a couple, indicating a growing capacity to resolve conflicts.

Relationship to the Environment
At the time of Andrew's death, both Sarah and David's links with their own families of origin were very tenuous. But since that time, Sarah had re-established contact with her own family. There was some evidence, however, that the alliance between David and his mother was still a source of marital conflict. The family had moved a number of times, so that links with the neighbourhood were restricted. Despite previous suspicions and difficulties connected with the taking of the care order and the police investigations following Joanne's abuse, the parents were beginning to make use of the foster parents and other professionals as a resource.

Focal assessment
Reviewing the current presenting problem and its links with the functioning of the family and the past history of the two parents, we arrived at a focal formulation. This is expressed in four steps:
a) *Symptom restated in interactional form* (How is the symptom linked to the family function?)

b) *Reframing the symptom* (What is the symptom's function and underlying meaning in the family?)

c) *Feared disaster and anxiety* (What would the family members worry about if the symptom was not present?)

d) *Link to original stressful experience* (Which past experience(s) is/are judged to be linked to the present family dysfunction?)

So that the formulation ran as follows:
(a) The abusive incident with Joanne occurred as a diversion from a barely contained resentment between the parents resulting from the disasters that had taken place during their recent past. (b) Joanne's subsequent removal into care activated Sarah and David's unresolved grief about Andrew's death and enabled them to support each other and also brought in the professional system, (c) thus avoiding the disaster of a total separation. Their positive links with the professional network, in particular Joanne's foster parents and their current social worker, acted as a counter-balance to (d) David's own family's pattern of avoiding conflict, reflected in his mother's family rule, 'All for one and one for all', and Sarah's experience in her family of origin of her mother being ill and of being sexually abused and having resorted to drug abuse and forgery as a way of dealing with pain and loss. This

particular combination of factors resulted in a silent, non-communicative marriage marked with sporadic explosions and violence.

This formulation indicated that for rehabilitation to occur safely, this couple would need to be able to learn to communicate painful reactions and feelings without recourse to silence, diversion to drugs or anti-social behaviour or marital violence. They should also be able to manage stressful times in the care of Joanne. This should be achieved by maintaining their links with the foster parents and continuing their work on their feelings of grief and blame about both Andrew's death and Joanne's abuse.

Conclusion

Assessing parenting capacity and making a recommendation about what is in a child's best interest is one of the most painful and difficult tasks a professional has to perform. In order to avoid being caught up into seeing the problem entirely from the viewpoint of either the parent or child, or being pulled from one to the other, the professional needs to have a series of frameworks with which to work. We have suggested that these need to include some ways of describing the day-to-day life of the child, including his or her physical and emotional care. Parenting must also be put into the context of the way the family functions as a whole, and we have delineated some key dimensions of family life and described break-down states for these dimensions. Through a case example we have attempted to show how the problem of a child being physically abused can be linked with the level of living provided for the child, characteristic patterns of family interaction and stressful past events.

Such an assessment should also help the professional to pinpoint strengths as well as weaknesses in the family and to specify what changes need to be achieved if the child's safety and/or satisfactory development is to be ensured. If such changes cannot be achieved, the professional then has a comprehensive assessment of the situation on which to make a decision to propose that alternative family care is necessary.

References

Fahlberg V
(1981) *Attachment and separation.* BAAF.

Kinston W and Bentovim A
(1982) 'Constructing a focal formulation and hypothesis in family therapy'. *Australian Journal of Family Therapy* 4 1 37-50.

Loader P et al
(1981) 'A method for organizing the clinical description of family interaction: the "family interaction summary format".' *Australian Journal of Family Therapy* 2 3 131-141.

Polansky N A, Chalmers M A, Buttenwieser E and Williams D P (1981) *Damaged parents: an anatomy of neglect.* Chicago: University of Chicago Press.

'Good-enough', border-line and 'bad-enough' parenting

Christine Cooper

Dr Cooper is Honorary Consultant Paediatrician, Newcastle General Hospitals and Medical Adviser to Newcastle-upon-Tyne Borough Council.

Parent-child relationships and the early development

The human infant is the most immature and dependent newborn of all species and remains relatively dependent longer than others. Without a caring adult the infant would die and so mothering has to do with survival of the species as well as of the individual. The basis for the baby's early emotional experiences is the mother's built-in drive to nurture and protect her infant, who develops and matures in the reciprocal relationship with his mother. Although mothering is rooted in physiological states, the mother is more independent of preformed instinctual patterns than other species, leaving her freer to adapt to her own child's needs. Socio-cultural traditions, poor role-models or psychological stress may limit her behaviour. The biological roots of fatherhood lie in the instinctual drive for survival through producing a child of his own sex.

Parenthood develops and unfolds alongside the development of the children, and preparation for this important role was once acquired in childhood and adolescence by living in large families. Research has shown that training and preparation for childbirth and the early weeks of parenthood helps to promote spontaneous delivery and enhances the parents' feelings for the newborn child and their willingness to be fully involved with his care. *Bonding* is the word that has been used for the parents' feelings and capacity to nurture which blossom over the early months.

In describing the importance of early development and nurturing Anna Freud (1970) points out that 'all advantages of a later family life may be wasted on a child who has lacked a warm and satisfying mother relationship in the first instance... In this earliest partnership the demands are all on one side (the infant's), while the obligations are all on the other (the mother's)... If she proves a gratifying and accommodating provider for his pressing needs, he begins to love, not only his experiences of wish fulfilment, but her person. Thereby the infant's original stage of self-centredness is changed into an attitude of emotional interest in his environment, and he becomes capable of loving, first the mother and – after her – the father and other important figures in his external world. . . The relationship of a mother to her infant is an exacting one.'

Attachment has come to mean the child's feelings for his mother and later other family members. His attachment to his main care-giver, usually his mother, is the basis for all future relationships. If it is very full of conflict he may find it hard to form other satisfying relationships.

Biological potential and the facilitating environment

Every child is born with the biological potential for growth and development. The environment in which the child is nurtured determines whether this potential is reached in adulthood and the parents and family life of the child are the most important part of this environment. Various research studies have confirmed this, (Martin 1976), especially those concerning very small, ill, or handicapped children (Neligan et al 1976, Rutter and Hersov 1984).

Some people do not reach their full potential in all aspects of development and may have dormant skills which are not fully realised. Some develop these in later life perhaps following unemployment, retirement or illness. But in general parents provide their children with 'good-enough' care and training and give them opportunities to develop their many skills, usually encouraged and assisted by educators in various settings.

Most parents are 'good-enough', a term Winnicott (1965, page 145) used to indicate that 'perfect parents' do not exist. 'Good-enough' parents bring up their children with success and enjoyment, even though most families meet some hard times on the way. Thus parents provide a 'facilitating environment' (Winnicott 1965, page 223) for each child to promote his development by their sensitivity and awareness of the child's needs. Essentially this means that parents adapt their behaviour and lifestyle as far as possible for the child's well-being rather than their own and they try to put the child's needs first in all major family plans and decisions. Ordinary parents discuss their children's needs from time to time and plan for them together, and in doing so they sometimes seek advice from professionals and others.

The purpose of the family

Spence (1946) set out the four main purposes of the family and emphasised, as educators do today, that no other human institution is so adequate in nurturing the growing child.

The four purposes are:

a) to promote growth and physical health

b) to provide scope for emotional experience

c) to preserve the art of motherhood

d) to teach behaviour

Parenting is a hard task as well as being enjoyable and producing feelings of fulfilment in the parents. In complex western societies, with intricate laws and rules, it is an advantage, both for parents and their children, when parenthood is postponed beyond the teenage years, to allow for increased maturity and general knowledge in tackling the difficult tasks of nurturing the next generation.

The child's basic needs

Many educators, psychologists and others have described the child's needs which 'good-enough' parents meet, largely intuitively, because of their affection and concern for the child. For example, see Pringle (1975). These can be summarised for all cultures as follows:

a) *basic physical care* which includes warmth, shelter, adequate food and rest, grooming (hygiene) and protection from danger

b) *affection* which includes physical contact, holding, stroking, cuddling and kissing, comforting, admiration, delight, tenderness, patience, time, making allowances for annoying behaviour, general companionship and approval

c) *security* which involves:
continuity of care
the expectation of continuing in the stable family unit
a predictable environment
consistent patterns of care and daily routine
simple rules and consistent controls
a harmonious family group

d) *stimulation of innate potential* by praise, by encouraging curiosity and exploratory behaviour, by developing skills through responsiveness to questions and to play, by promoting educational opportunities

e) *guidance and control* to teach adequate social behaviour which includes discipline within the child's understanding and capacity, and which requires patience and a model for the child to copy, for example in honesty and concern and kindness for others

f) *responsibility* for small things at first such as self-care, tidying play things or taking dishes to the kitchen, and gradually elaborating the decision-making the child has to learn in order to function adequately, gaining experience through his mistakes as well as his successes, and receiving praise and encouragement to strive and do better

g) *independence* to make his own decisions, first about small things, but increasingly about the various aspects of his life within the confines of the family and society's codes. Parents use fine judgement in encouraging independence, and in letting the child see and feel the outcome of his own poor judgement and mistakes, but within the compass of his capacity. Protection is needed, but over-protection is as bad as too early responsibility and independence.

The early stages of development

The parents' main achievement in the early months is promoting the sense of basic trust in the infant as the foundation of sound personality development (Erikson 1950). By being available and being responsive to the infant's needs, and by providing a stable home and a predictable environment, parents enable the baby to learn to trust them. At the same time the sense of self emerges in the baby and self-confidence develops as the baby and toddler learns to seek and receive comfort in predictable ways. He becomes deeply attached to his main care-givers and through them the urgent drives of the early years are fulfilled. These are to explore, to achieve mastery and status and to seek companionship. Encouragement and provision of a safe environment for his developing skills further promotes his self-confidence and self-esteem and pandering to his need for attachment in the early years pays dividends in a more secure and confident child later (Bowlby 1979, Parkes et al 1982).

As time goes on his growing understanding and the mastery of skills in the basic tasks of independent living together with his slowly developing time concepts allow him to venture forth safely from the shelter of his family to increasing degrees as the years go by. The proximity of his family and their understanding of his needs and temperament, their patience, encouragement and controls, continue to be important for the child's optimum development. The parents modify and organise the child's environment as far as they are able in keeping with his developmental requirements.

'Good-enough' parents show pride and pleasure in their child's progress together with many other positive emotions such as affection, tenderness, interest, delight and many others which increase the child's self-confidence and self-esteem. There are also, at times, negative feelings towards their children such as frustration, fatigue, anger, boredom, anxiety, fear, disappointment and many others, which parents learn to accept as normal when occurring only occasionally. Professionals concerned with families such as doctors, health visitors, teachers and social workers, need understanding and awareness of when the negative feelings are becoming excessive and when they may swamp the positive ones. Then various ways to relieve these stresses need discussion with the family and sometimes further professional help.

Cultural and class perspectives

There is considerable variation in child rearing beliefs and practices and what one group considers 'good-enough' another may regard as damaging and abusive. For example, western cultures condemn the pain, fear and mutilation involved in many tribal initiation practices at puberty, while those who practise them regard the western parents' belief in allowing a baby to cry without immediately comforting it or the practice of isolating a baby to sleep in his own room as equally barbarous. Understanding the implications of the practices themselves and of stopping them are often lacking. For example, without the signs (eg facial scarifications) that initiation has taken place an individual can become an outcast in his own society. Changes come with education and increasing knowledge but they are slow as each society adapts to new conditions.

On another level, the same practice in different cultural contexts may also have very different effects on children. For example, sibling care-taking in the context of a traditional village community, with no traffic or major environmental hazards, and with supportive adults nearby, is very different from the western model in unsafe urban estates and houses, with traffic, fire, electricity and other hazards and with parents at work or leisure very far away and no other adults with responsibility around.

When it comes to discipline and the use of physical punishment or restraints, opinions across cultures, and even within a culture, vary widely, for example whether hitting children for discipline is wise or harmful and what limits should be set. However, there seems to be general agreement across cultures that children should not be injured by any of these practices although what is considered an injury is also sometimes debatable. Most cultures have prescribed rules for discipline, and for other child rearing practices and these take note of harm to a child which prevents his development (Korbin 1979, 1981).

One sometimes hears a professional say that another professional is judging parental practices by middle class standards, yet most 'good-enough' parents agree about what constitutes 'good-enough' care and control. Polansky and his colleagues (1981, Chapter 6) have recently highlighted this and found that there are no significant class differences on this important topic, anyhow in a North American urban society.

Perhaps the key feature in assessing whether practices are harmful to children is to consider whether they harm the child's growth and development and whether they belittle or denigrate his self-image. The behaviour, not the child, should be the cause for correction and if the child feels the correction or punishment is fair, and that all other children in his society face similar correction, it is probably not harmful. The scapegoated child who is singled out for condemnation and/or drudgery is the damaged one who may end up with burning resentment and anger which every now and then explodes and which is a constrictive force in his relationships and overall functioning as an adult.

Severe parenting problems

When parents are having problems in coping with their children it is important to look for the possible causes and to remember the very complex problems in abusive families. Sometimes a temporary upset from family illness, accident, unemployment etc. clears up as soon as the cause is resolved. Most families meet adversity and develop coping skills. In some families, however, episodes of distress may follow each other in quick succession until things get out of hand and one or both parents feel swamped by the complexity of the problems. The skills they do have can become submerged in all the anxiety and effort to cope, and the children's development and well-being may suffer in many different ways. (Straus 1980, Steele 1980)

Child abuse and neglect is the end of the spectrum of parenting difficulties, and awareness on the part of professionals such as health visitors, doctors, teachers and social workers, that a family is moving to that end of the parenting spectrum, increasingly results in assessment and help before abuse and neglect occur. The causes are complex and the words 'wilful' or 'deliberate' to describe parental actions are seldom appropriate. Most abusive parents have experienced the breaking of affectional bonds, often repeatedly, and some have scarcely developed such bonds in the first place (Bowlby 1979).

Origin of parental problems
The origins of parental problems can be summarised under six headings and usually a complex variety of difficulties are summated for any family. Awareness of a family's vulnerability and loads of stress in these various areas can assist professionals to determine which families need extra time and help.

1. Vulnerability to parenting problems
Research increasingly shows that parents' behaviour with their children tends to repeat the patterns of behaviour and attitudes

which their own parents used with them (Oliver & Taylor 1971, Oliver & Cox 1973, Oliver 1983). A harsh, neglectful or otherwise unsatisfactory upbringing experienced by themselves makes it hard for parents, in many ways, to empathise with their children and to show the necessary awareness, patience and tenderness, and the ability to put the child's needs before their own. Most abusing and neglectful parents do love their children but they are sad people who lacked adequate affection, interest and concern when young and they are now swamped by their excessive need for these supports in adult life. Deprived parents may look to their children to supply affection, understanding and support, and this role-reversal may be very marked. Such parents remain unhappy and frustrated when they experience the impossibility of the child fulfilling their needs. 'Assortive' matings, when 'like' partners 'like' and two deprived people produce children, further complicates the picture.

It is interesting that research in many areas (Martin 1976, especially chapter 2, and Farrington 1978) has consistently shown that the most damaging aspects of the home environment as far as aggressive tendencies and delinquency go are:

a) indifference and coldness towards the child's needs and interests, in some cases progressing to rejection

b) severe physical punishment

c) persistent parental discord

Polansky (1981) has described the aftermath of severe neglect. Kempe (1980) and Harris (1982) among many others have described the problems in families with children who fail to thrive (ie who have psycho-social dwarfism). Wolkind and his team in London are studying a longitudinal sample of unselected British mothers having their first babies which are then followed up for health, growth, development, behaviour and learning for the first five years. Interesting differences in patterns of mothering are revealed early on, which largely depend on the mother's own experiences while growing up (eg Hall et al 1979).

2. Bonding problems
As we have seen, parents begin to form their relationship with the child during pregnancy and this gradually increases at birth and in the early days, weeks and months of life as the parents respond to and nurture their helpless infant. Closeness of mother and infant in the days and weeks following birth promotes their understanding and their mutual responses and the development of their reciprocal relationship, so getting them off to a good start. The father's role is also enhanced by early involvement (Ounsted et al 1974, Klaus and Kennell 1982).

Difficulties or illness in mother or baby during pregnancy, around the time of birth or in the early months of life can frustrate the parents' awareness, sensitivity and responses to the baby's needs. Parents with adequate parenting skills usually overcome such difficulties later on although some remain aware of the subtle effects of these early problems on their subsequent relationship with the child. Parents, already more vulnerable to problems by virtue of their own difficult upbringing, may lack the capacity to develop adequate nurturing for a child when illness and separation have complicated the early weeks. This may set in train a pattern of parenting in which coldness and indifference develop and then neglect or physical attacks may occur in a few cases (Lynch 1975).

3. Family difficulties
There is often discord between the partners because each is so needful of sympathy and support for themselves they are unable to see the other's needs or the helplessness or the immaturity of the baby and young child. In addition there may be other family problems and discord, with illness or poor relationships especially with their own parents. 'Hostile dependency' with parents or siblings is distressingly common.

4. Ill-health
Health problems, especially in the mother, are often added to the other stresses and make her task of family management even harder. Rather than major health problems these are often a combination of minor disorders such as anaemia, bladder or gynaecological problems, headaches, toothache, ear problems, foot problems and minor skin disorders. Worries over contraception may be added to the list of difficulties which can undermine even a competent housewife and mother.

Depression is very common too and sometimes an agitated anxiety state occurs. Doctors need to be wary in prescribing tranquillisers which may enhance the tendency to violence by inhibiting controls. It is crucial for professionals to assess such health problems and treat them very carefully.

5. An unresolved loss
The loss of a parent or other child or of some other relative can produce significant psychological stress when the 'grief-work' and mourning has been incomplete. This occurs especially where a degree of closeness is mingled with hostility or where a child has died or has been relinquished or removed from the family without adequate expression of feelings. (Derivan 1982)

6. Social problems
An additional load of stress comes from poor housing, overcrowding,

poverty, too frequent child-bearing, alcohol and drug abuse, gambling, sub-normality, criminality, mental illness and many other disorders in the social environment. Clearly improving housing and financial resources, neighbourhood recreation and other social facilities would go a long way to helping families although these are not the basic problems.

Assessing parental capacity

Observation of family interaction together with measurements of the child's growth and development and social adaptations are the main tools for understanding parental competence. Household hygiene and management, including food and meals, regular bedtime, provision for play and reading stories, together with the family's functioning in the local society are additional means of assessment. A family without friends and support is usually very vulnerable.

Repeated observations of mother/infant interactions in the early weeks give a trained observer important knowledge about their developing relationship and the ability of the mother to nurture and protect her child adequately in the future. The effect of the infant's behaviour on the mother's responses needs assessment and in particular careful recognition of the few infants who are tense, unable to cuddle-in at first, tend to arch themselves backwards or to have problems in feeding in the early weeks. A confident and competent mother may not be disarmed by such a baby and in a few weeks things start going well. An inexperienced and vulnerable girl, on the other hand, may be severely taxed, and the process of bonding over the early months, with the development of tenderness and sensitivity, is delayed or distorted, in the struggle to achieve a reciprocal relationship and a contented child (Lewis and Rosenblum 1974, Frude 1980, Fraiberg 1980, Harris 1982, Evler 1982).

Parent/infant interaction

Since the mother usually has the main task of mothering and early nurturing the descriptions refer to her, but fathers too can experience similar reactions.

1. Favourable signs in the early months
Signs that the relationship is starting well (assuming a full-term healthy baby) are:

a) the establishment of mutual gaze from birth onwards, momentarily at first and then for increasing periods

b) mutual smiling from 4 – 6 weeks old and occasionally earlier

c) reciprocal vocalisations from 6 – 8 weeks old

d) crying which quietens, momentarily in the early weeks, at the mother's voice, touch or holding

e) snuggling-in comfortably together

f) satisfactory feeding and sleep and a contented, thriving baby

g) adequate hygiene and skin care for the baby

h) 'awareness' by the mother and appropriate responses to the baby's signals

i) the mother's obvious pleasure and delight with the baby's growth and development, expressed in words or gestures and later in play. This is sometimes mingled with temporary anxiety which occurs from time to time in all normal families.

2. Favourable signs in the later months and toddler years

a) *in play with the mother's clothes and body* From 3 or 4 months the baby normally enjoys playing with the mother's face, hair, necklace, clothes or hands during feeding and care-giving, and the child seeks the mother's gaze and response with his eyes and vocalisations.

b) *referencing back during play* When mobile he enjoys exploring, but frequently refers back to his mother by glance, vocalisations or touch. From 8 or 9 months onwards for the next 2 or 3 years he may be uneasy when his mother leaves him and actively seek reunion. This attachment behaviour lessens over the years.

c) *interactive games* From about 8 months onwards the baby enjoys interactive games with his parents and other familiar people in which he gradually learns a part such as peep bo, hand-and-face or give-and-take games and many others. The baby becomes insatiable for the enjoyment these bring and his demands captivate friendly adults around him.

d) *general liveliness and exploring behaviour* From 6 or 7 months onwards the cherished baby is full of vigour, liveliness and movement and any new sound, object or place is avidly explored. His mother watches for dangerous situations and thinks ahead to keep him safe. She trains him gradually about things he may or may not touch by telling him in words while cheerfully removing him from the object. Later on, words alone will be enough.

e) *stranger anxiety* From 7 or 8 months onwards anxiety is seen at a stranger's approach and may be intense for a few weeks. There-after for the next 2 or 3 years, sometimes more, a child is reserved with strangers until he has summed them up and decided whether responding to their approaches would be safe and interesting. Some children by temperament are more reserved than others.

When these favourable signs are absent or muted, and when anxiety and frustration predominates in the mother, or negativism in the baby, early recognition of these difficulties should lead to assessment of their causes and the provision of extra help and support for the family. The aim is to prevent harmful methods of child rearing growing out of the early problems.

Worrying interactions and behaviour in infants and young children

If difficulties in mother/infant or father/infant interaction are not resolved, either spontaneously or with professional help, they may progress to patterns of behaviour which are increasingly negative in both parent and child and when negative reinforcement plays a part in the vicious circle which develops. The child's expectations and behaviour then becomes distorted and disturbed.

Some negative interactions can be seen in all families at times when child or parents are tired or when preoccupation and other worries temporarily upset or dampen the parents' normal responses. Children's resilience quickly overcomes such temporary disorders. It is important to confirm that the behaviour is persistent before initiating a detailed assessment, although discussion of possible problems with the mother and improved ways of handling the baby will usually have begun before this. Discussion of the parents' feelings and their sense of inadequacy and hopelessness is just as important. This can assail even very good parents, briefly, at times.

The following worrying behaviour may be seen in babies and toddlers and, if persistent and if several are present, should give cause for concern that the child's development may be severely damaged. Such a child and family should always be referred for assessment to a suitable paediatric or child psychiatry clinic.

1. In the early months
a) *gaze avoidance,* in which the baby, from about 3 or 4 months onwards, turns away to avoid the gaze of one or other parent. Head turning may accompany this.

b) *smiling is fleeting or muted* instead of joyous and exuberant

c) *lack of liveliness and withdrawal* in which it is hard to catch the baby's attention

d) *inability to cuddle-in* or to be easily comforted by the parent's voice or by feeding, holding, rocking or play

e) *poor feeding and sleep* although these may have organic causes at times

f) *persistent vomiting or loose stools,* or other bodily symptoms, all of which may sometimes have organic causes and a doctor with special experience of infants should keep such a family under careful surveillance

g) *failure to grow and develop well,* without medical (organic) causes

h) *inadequate hygiene and skin care* with persistent nappy rash

2. In the older baby and toddler
Any of the above signs may be seen and in addition:

i) *self comforting* by rocking, excessive thumb sucking or masturbation

j) *signs of frustration* such as head banging, hair pulling, hand biting and other self-injuring behaviour

k) *frozen watchfulness or hyper-vigilance* in which a child watches an approaching adult with caution to see what mood they are in. Ducking or face-shielding to avoid blows may be seen in toddlers or older children

l) *lack of liveliness and exploratory behaviour* with objects or with the environment

m) *anxious attachment,* recognised by excessive attention and affection-seeking behaviour and persistently anxious clinging to the parent or others

n) *'promiscuousness'* in seeking attention indiscriminately from strangers without the usual shyness or initial reserve

o) *not 'referencing-back'* to the care-giver by glance, vocalisation, touch or the initiating of cuddling

p) *not seeking comfort* when hurt or distressed

q) *wailing 'hopeless' crying* with little expectation of relief

r) *persistent disobedience* and negativism

s) *chaotic, hyper-active play* with little concentration or attention span. (Occasionally an organic basis exists for this.)

t) *persistent disturbances in bodily functions* such as eating, sleeping and toileting

u) *pseudo-mature behaviour* and role reversal in which the child is oversensitive to parental distress and offers comfort or placating behaviour inappropriately for his age

Worrying behaviour and attitudes of parents

In the families we are concerned about, these signs in the child are usually accompanied by negative attitudes in the parents, including some of the following:

a) *coercive intervention* with too frequent 'orders' given to a little child without time, patience and coaxing to obtain his compliance

b) *frequent smacking* especially of babies and toddlers, usually for things the child does not understand

c) *carelessness about the whereabouts and safety* of young children

d) *unfeeling attitudes* and frustrating the young child's ordinary behaviour in play and exploring; not providing alternative interesting objects and occupations when a dangerous one has to be removed or terminated

e) *unreal expectations* of behaviour and obedience and little praise and encouragement

f) *role-reversal* – expecting care and comfort from small children

g) *severe physical discipline* and *cruel punishments* such as locking-up, drudgery, deprivation of food, warmth or companionship etc

h) *hostile remarks or gestures* with frequent denigration and disparagement of all the child's effort. This breaks his trust and damages his self-esteem, the two basic developmental achievements necessary in the early years

i) *imputing an infant's reflex behaviour* such as vomiting or passing a stool, or even wetting the nappy, as done deliberately to annoy the parent

j) *persistent discord between the parents* or with other family members together with frequent violence or arguments

Overall family functioning

As the children grow, looking at parent/child relationships as well as an assessment of the overall pattern of family functioning and relationships is important. These include looking at alliances, discipline, scape-goating, decision-making, handling conflicts, the attitudes of the extended family, the neighbourhood network, and many other parameters of family life.

The abusive environment

It can be seen then that the abusive environment and disordered parenting has a marked effect on the child's development and is far more serious for his eventual personality growth than the occasional bruises, burns or fractures which occur from time to time in abusive families, damaging though these certainly are. The injuries are one pointer to the unsatisfactory home. Permanent damage to personality will handicap the child throughout his life (Martin 1976, especially chapter 2).

When the environment involves failure to meet the baby's early needs for feeding and care the infant fails to thrive and develop. Older children may fail to thrive too, when depressed and unhappy, but this early sign is often missed because adequate checks on growth and development are not made and charted.

In the second and third years the damaged parent's lack of awareness of a child's limited development and understanding leads them to expect too much from the child in obedience and conformity. The parents issue orders instead of coaxing the toddler towards desirable behaviour. When he fails to comply he is slapped and shouted at and this soon produces negativism, tantrums and disobedience and so a vicious circle results. Hostility from the parents may follow with frequent belittling, sarcasm and unfair treatment. Cruel punishment and physical abuse may then occur and the parents sometimes come to see the child as bad and worthless. Often the child believes he is so and his self-concept is permanently warped. 'Marked deprivation' can occur when many 'compensatory' services are provided for the family or child in the neighbourhood (family aide, nursery place, etc) so that the child thrives better although his emotional needs for a warm attachment for encouragement, praise and recognition are not being met and personality handicap is the result. Skill is needed to know when the compensation is not enough in any individual case.

Another dimension of child abuse and parenting problems is the sexual abuse of children. This may occur within the family, or outside it from friends or acquaintances, and very rarely from a stranger. Boys are molested as well as girls. In extra-familial cases the child is usually vulnerable and needy of extra affection and attention or is badly supervised. Space does not permit further comment but knowledge and publications are growing fast. (Kempe and Kempe 1978, chapter 4, for a brief account, or Mrazek and Kempe 1981)

Professionals still have a great deal to learn about how best to help these families, and the criteria on which one can be sure that improvement in parenting will not occur, or not in time for the particular child's needs. Permanent placement away from the biological family is clearly indicated for some of these children.

Very detailed assessments over time, and with careful consideration of all the aspects of family life, need to be made before taking such a decision, which, in any case, should rarely be made or confirmed outside a case conference of senior experienced personnel from the relevant disciplines.

Effects on the child of abuse and neglect

Although some parents abuse and neglect their children, most of them do so despite their efforts to provide adequate care. Their own personality problems and distorted life experiences make nurturing children very hard for them, swamped as they are by their own need for appreciation and care. Marked physical injuries (non-accidental injuries) are probably the least common form of abuse, whereas neglect and emotional abuse are much more common and, it is now realised, sexual abuse is also very common. 'Good-enough' parents can avoid these problems because of sounder personality functioning.

It is important to remember the damage which results when parenting is not 'good-enough', and this is an incentive to learning more about early recognition and about developing the skills to help parents and children before it is too late.

The effects of an environment which is not 'good-enough', and may even be abusive, can be summarised thus:

a) *death* from physical injuries or from gross failure to thrive. Milder cases of poor growth may be associated with unhappiness and proneness to succumb to infections. The death certificate may only record the infection.

b) *damage* which is permanent, to the brain, eyes, hearing, joints, skin or internal organs as a result of injury, with or without malnutrition

c) *deprivation dwarfism* (failure to thrive) from inadequate nutrition and care

d) *disturbance* in personality development of mild, moderate or severe degree, from the psychological stresses of the abusive environment

e) *delay in cognitive development* and learning capacity with poor concentration and short attention span

f) *delay in language and speech development* usually associated with poor concentration, poor abstract reasoning, constriction of imaginative ideas and originality

g) *distorted perception* of people and relationships and the way the world functions

h) *demanding behaviour* and over-activity

i) *dependency* from having failed to develop adequate self-confidence, drive and initiative due to poor nurture in the early months and to persistent belittling or lack of suitable praise or encouragement

j) *delinquency* with varying degrees of disobedience, defiance and aggressiveness

k) *detachment* from lack of continuous affectionate and reliable relationships and usually stemming from multiple moves and caretakers in the early years. Those in whom this trait persists may become the affectionless psychopaths of the next generation, some of whom will be violent and commit murder, rape and other brutal crimes.

Many individuals as a result of the abusive environment in which they grow up suffer several of these handicaps and could be a constant drain on society in the future, being largely unemployable and being frequent inmates of mental hospitals or prisons.

Some permanent personality handicaps

The traits we see developing in children from an abusive environment present as personality handicaps as the children reach adulthood and some in turn become abusing parents in the next generation. The degree and varieties of handicap vary but in some individuals they severely impair family life and general functioning in society. The next generation of children then become affected.

The more important personality handicaps are listed below; the first two are universal and most deprived individuals have several, while in the more severely and persistently abused they show nearly all these characteristics:

a) *lack of trust* which makes it hard for them to see professionals as helpful

b) *poor self-esteem* and self-confidence

c) *feeling laden with guilt* and badness from the constant denigration making it hard for them to believe people could find them worthy of help or esteem

d) *having yearnings for affection* and going from one liaison to another in an attempt, usually fruitless, to fill the void within

e) *being unable to 'give'* in a relationship, so needy are they to 'receive' affection and attention

f) *impulsiveness*, wanting immediate gratification of their wishes as in young children. The ability to plan and think ahead to the consequences of such actions is severely limited. Feelings are translated into actions as in a young child, and they have not learnt that we have a right to our feelings (rage, joy, etc) but must temper their expression, using words rather than actions

g) *selfishness and self-centred attitudes* because they have become accustomed to having to fend for themselves due to lack of adequate parental concern

h) *self-righteousness* to justify their various behaviours

i) *self-destructiveness*, with suicide attempts

j) *denial of problems* and living in a precarious balance with reality, because to face the difficulties might lead to personality disintegration and breakdown. This is an important point to remember in treatment.

k) *suspiciousness* and paranoid feelings

l) *outbursts of rage and anger* against unfairness and perceived persecution

It can be seen why abusing parents have such difficulties in accepting services and in recognising offers of help as genuine and on their behalf.

Monitoring growth and development

As we increase our knowledge and understanding of 'good-enough' parenting and of the damage to children when parents are unable to be 'good-enough', we shall learn first to recognise the early stages and second to provide treatment and help for families before they reach the stage of 'no return'.

Thriving, contented children with acceptable social behaviour are one mark of 'good-enough' parenting, and assessment of a child's progress by measuring growth and development is one of the most effective ways of detecting problems early.

The following parameters of growth and development should be considered:

● *Physical* The increase in size and function

- *Sensory* The ability to use the five senses and interpret the sensory input

- *Intellectual* The ability to learn and to adapt behaviour appropriately

- *Emotional* The capacity to form relationships and to empathise

- *Social* The ability, first, for self-care, then appropriate social behaviour and later the ability to share in the work tasks of the community. Play is the 'work' of childhood through which children develop their skills, knowledge and social adaptation.

- *Moral* The knowledge of right and wrong through the child's developing conscience, and the ability to respect and be concerned for other people's persons, their property and their feelings.

We can measure physical growth and development accurately and compare this with the norms for the age, sex and society in which the child lives by charting the growth curves for height, weight and skull circumference. Development of motor, manipulative, visual, auditory, language and personal-social skills can also be more or less accurately assessed on the various scales available.

Sensory development has been largely neglected professionally and for deprived and disadvantaged children the deficits may be handicapping. Children may see but have not been taught 'to look properly', they may hear normally but have not been taught 'to listen', they may have a poor body image with resulting clumsiness, and they may be relatively unable to interpret the causes of common bodily sensations such as hunger, tiredness, thirst, colic, nausea, full bowel or bladder, etc.

Intellectual development and learning skills are also capable of accurate assessment and charting of progress, and knowledge in this sphere is increasing rapidly.

Emotional maturity is more difficult to assess accurately but considerable strides have been made in this sphere too in recent years, especially in assessments during the early years of development.

The social and adaptive behaviour can increasingly be compared with the norms for the cultural group and charted but this applies mainly to western societies so far.

Moral concepts are also capable of assessment and more notice needs to be taken of the development of these.

Paediatricians, psychologists, psychiatrists, teachers, speech therapists and social workers, among others, are those involved in these assessments and in observing a child's progress over time. The rate of growth and development under different conditions is an important part of the assessment.

Tools to work with

There is still a long way to go in learning the professional tasks in assessing parenting function through a multi-disciplinary team, but much headway has been made in recent years. The tools we have are being increasingly used for repeated family assessments in the delicate tasks of deciding when for any child or family, the parenting is not 'good-enough' in spite of help and guidance or special treatments. The child may then have to be removed. The dilemma for the professionals is that leaving a child in a damaging atmosphere may do irreparable harm to his personality, and yet all wish to give parents the benefit of the doubt and more time, in the hope that they can acquire the skills to nurture their children effectively. In the present climate, too many children are probably left in severely damaging homes.

The main tools are:

a) regular measurements of growth and development including school and social progress

b) assessment of parent/child relationships and general family function

c) providing suitable treatments for parents and child, and training and support for parents and family in improved methods of child care, based on understanding the child's needs at varying ages. Voluntary support groups may help some families

d) being alert to the early danger signs of abnormal behaviour in children or parents and applying assessment and treatment early with regular re-assessment of progress

e) regular meetings of the involved professionals to discuss progress and to plan more effective treatment, which in a few means removal of the child, temporarily or permanently

f) the use of legal controls to protect the child and increase parental incentives where these are lacking

g) assessment of the child's growth and development in a therapeutic environment when progress at home is severely restricted. If the child improves and this is not maintained on one return home, serious consideration should be given to permanent placement in a substitute family

h) removal of the child to permanent substitute family care, usually
as a last resort, when in spite of help the family is unable to
provide parenting on which the child can thrive. In a few cases
this diagnosis is made when the family is first seen.

Compassion versus control

All 'good-enough' parents exert affection, compassion and control to
promote their child's progress to maturity. With damaged parents,
whose own growth on many parameters has been distorted and
restricted, introducing legal controls can often be an incentive to
more effective collaboration and care of their children and the use of
services which will help them in providing family functioning.

One of the most important tasks for professionals is learning how to
use authority on the one hand, to ensure the child's welfare (and
legal controls for many families will be a necessary part of this), and
on the other hand to remain encouraging and supportive to the
family, keeping them motivated to improve (Rosenfeld and
Newberger 1979, Bourne and Newberger 1979).

Only as a last resort, in our culture, do we plan to remove children,
and perhaps we need to develop skills to help more parents
relinquish them earlier when their problems are overwhelming. For
the children, too, have rights, to grow and develop their potential as
healthy members of a society. 'Divorce' between parents and
children needs to be used as a tool of communication, without laying
blame on the parents. Some parents would willingly relinquish if it
were not for other relatives' or neighbours' caustic remarks.

A major problem in the compassion/control controversy is failure to
realise how damaged in their concepts many of these parents are.
Because of the personality traits already mentioned they find it hard
to believe we value them and are concerned for their welfare as well
as the child's. Support is needed in the Juvenile Court and much
help and support for those families who do have children removed.
They tend to view this as a punishment rather than as a means of
providing adequate care for the child, and also a way of removing
intolerable stresses in themselves. Some parents, in a year or two, can
recognise this and approve of the chance of a better life for their child.

References

Bourne R and Newberger E H
(1979) ' "Family autonomy" or "co-ercive intervention" ' in
R Bourne and E H Newberger (eds) *Critical perspectives on child
abuse*. Lexington, Massachusetts: Lexington Books.

Bowlby J
(1979) *The making and breaking of affectional bonds* (especially lectures 4 and 7). Tavistock Publications.

Derivan A T
(1982) 'Disorders of bonding' in P J Accado (ed) *Failure to thrive in infancy and early childhood.* Baltimore: University Park Press.

Evler G L
(1982) 'Non-medical management of the failure to thrive child in a paediatric inpatient setting' in P J Accado (ed) *Failure to thrive in infancy and early childhood.* Baltimore: University Park Press.

Erikson E H
(1950) *Childhood and society* (chapter 7). Penguin Books.

Farringdon D P
(1978) 'The family backgrounds of aggressive youths' in L A Hersov and M Berger *Aggressive and anti-social behaviour in childhood and adolescence.* Pergamon Press.

Fraiberg S (ed)
(1980) *Clinical studies in infant mental health* (especially chapter VII). Tavistock Publications.

Freud A
(1970) 'The concept of the rejecting mother' in E J Anthony and T Benedek (eds) *Parenthood: its psychology and psychopathology.* Boston: Little Brown and Company (and Churchill Ltd).

Frude N (ed)
(1980) *Psychological approaches to child abuse* (especially chapters 2 to 5 and chapters 7 and 8). Batsford Academic and Educational Ltd.

Hall F, Pawlby S J and Wolkind S
(1979) 'Early life experiences and later mothering behaviour' in D Shaffer and J Dunn (eds) *The first year of life.* John Wiley & Sons.

Harris J C
(1982) 'Non-organic failure to thrive syndromes' in P J Accado (ed) *Failure to thrive in infancy and early childhood.* Baltimore: University Park Press.

Kempe R S, Cutler C and Dean J
(1980) 'The infant with failure to thrive' in C H Kempe and R E Helfer (eds) *The battered child,* third edition. Chicago and London: University of Chicago Press.

Kempe R S and Kempe C H
(1978) *Child abuse.* Fontana Open Books.

Klaus M H and Kennell J H
(1982) *Parent-infant bonding,* second edition. C V Mosby Company.

Korbin J
(1979) 'A cross-cultural perspective on the role of the community in child abuse and neglect'. *Child Abuse: The International Journal* 3 (1) 9-18.
(1981) *Child abuse and neglect: cross-cultural perspectives.* Los Angeles: University of California Press.

Lewis M and Rosenblum L A (eds)
(1974) *The effect of the infant on its caregiver* (especially chapter 3). John Wiley & Sons Ltd.

Lynch M
(1975) 'Ill-health and child abuse'. *Lancet* 2.317.

Martin H P and Kempe C H (eds)
(1976) *The abused child.* Cambridge Massachusetts: Ballinger Publishing Company.

Mrazek P B and Kempe C H
(1981) *Sexually abused children and their families.* Pergamon Press.

Neligan G A, Scott D Mcl, Kolvin I and Garside R
(1976) *Born too soon or born too small* (especially pages 91 to 93). Spastics International Medical Publications, Lavenham Press.

Oliver J E
(1983) 'Dead children from problem families in N.E. Wiltshire'. *British Medical Journal* 286.115.

Oliver J E and Cox J
(1973) 'A family kindred with ill-used children: the burden on the community'. *British Journal of Psychiatry* 123.81.

Oliver J E and Taylor A
(1971) 'Five generations of ill-treated children in one family pedigree'. *British Journal of Psychiatry* 119.473.

Ounsted C, Oppenheimer R and Lindsay J
(1974) 'Aspects of bonding failure'. *Developmental Medicine and Child Neurology* 16.446.

Parkes C M and Stevenson Hinde J (eds)
(1982) *The place of attachment in human behaviour.* Tavistock Publications.

Polansky N A, Chalmers M A, Buttenwieser E and Williams D P
(1981) *Damaged parents: an anatomy of neglect.* Chicago: University of Chicago Press.

Pringle M K
(1975) *The needs of children.* Hutchinson Educational Ltd.

Rosenfeld A A and Newberger E H
(1979) 'Compassion versus control: conceptual and practical pitfalls in the broadened definition of child abuse' in R Bourne and E H

Newberger (eds) *Critical perspectives on child abuse.* Lexington, Massachusetts: Lexington Books.

Rutter M and Herson L
(1984) *Child and adolescent psychiatry: modern approaches* (especially chapters 3, 4 and 5). Blackwell Scientific.

Spence J C
(1946) *The purpose of the family: convocation lecture of the National Children's Home.* Epworth Press.

Steele B
(1980) 'Psychodynamic factors in child abuse' in C H Kempe and R E Helfer (eds) *The battered child,* third edition. Chicago and London: University of Chicago Press.

Straus M A
(1980) 'Stress and child abuse' in C H Kempe and R E Helfer (eds) *The battered child,* third edition. Chicago and London: University of Chicago Press.

Winnicott D W
(1965) *The maturational processes and the facilitative environment.* New York: International Universities Press.

Predicting a family's response to treatment

Robin Wratten

Robin Wratten is Project Leader, NSPCC Family Centre, Northamptonshire. The ideas discussed in this paper have developed from the author's experiences in rehabilitative work with families of physically abused and neglected children.

The work of Goldstein, Freud and Solnit (1973, 1980) has undoubtedly contributed to our knowledge concerning the return of children from care and the initial decision to remove. The concept of attachment is seen to have great importance. The dangers of damaging a relationship to a degree where it is irreparable (and the consequential damage and loss for some children) are clearly identified in many cases as greater than the likely outcome if they were left at home.

Inevitably, once a decision has been made to remove a child, families come under very close scrutiny and the standards expected of them before a child is returned may therefore be higher than those found in comparable families in the community. This is all the more significant when it is remembered that the majority of children in care come from the least affluent families and from strikingly disadvantaged backgrounds. Inevitably, professionals face dilemmas. Their observations are likely to be value laden and the time spent in deliberating over the return of the child may well be protracted. This may be very destructive to the already damaged attachment.

In order to cause as little damage as possible to relationships already impaired by the crisis, it is important to identify two key issues when a child is taken into care: the nature of the family crisis and the degree of family dysfunction.

Of course it would be better for all concerned if the social worker could consider the nature of the crisis and suggest ways of helping the family to cope. Reception into care would then not be necessary and the family would have learned to respond to stress in a constructive way.

Again, the work of Goldstein, Freud and Solnit is a useful reference as they identify two distinct responses to the question 'What should justify substituting the state's judgement for that of parents with regard to the care of a particular child?' They suggest that there are very clear and precise requirements in terms of what protection and physical care should be offered with regard to compulsory education, health care and what physical environment it is reasonable to expect. Secondly, however, is the area of neglect, both physical and emotional, which is not clearly defined and is veiled with such concepts as that the 'best interests of the child should be served'. Unfortunately this absence of definition inevitably results in subjective assessments and appraisals being made by primary workers on the basis of which children may well be removed. What is needed by all workers is an appreciation of what the consequences of their intervention in a particular family situation are likely to be and some guidelines as to what might best benefit the child in the long term.

Assessment of families

Central to any assessment of family functioning must be the consideration of its purpose. Characteristics of the families of children in care are often well understood. Mia Kellmer Pringle (1975) points to common features and there have also been extensive studies of predictive features in the field of child abuse or neglect, 'An obvious breakdown in the function of parenting' (Lynch and Roberts 1982).

What must concern us is whether there are certain features which would determine a specific approach to the family. Two studies of neglectful families have very similar findings, *The roots of futility* (Polansky 1972), a study of poor families from the Appalachian Mountains area in the US, and *Families without hope,* a study conducted in Sheffield by Tonge, James and Hillan (1975). Both the studies drew out features of the poor quality of life endured by the subjects and also the sense of apathy and futility which often pervades these families and threatens to overwhelm the inexperienced or unprepared worker who becomes involved. These studies more importantly give an insight into the families which puts them in a distinct category of need. The personalities of the parents are likely to be extremely immature, mothers are commonly described as infantile in character and the male members of the household are commonly assessed as 'unstable personalities'. It is also evident that adequate skills to respond to these families are frequently missing from the workers involved. The British study suggested that the special problems of these families were unsuited to the present social services departments: 'their long-term treatment should be regarded as a special responsibility of a few experienced case workers. When psychiatric help is needed this should be sought from a clinic where the staff are especially interested in this type of family and are prepared to make special arrangements for consultation and treatment, including domiciliary visits'.

In his study, Polansky used a technique of assessing the level of living that a child experienced. His questionnaire for the use of professionals is split into categories of physical care and emotional care. Each area is subdivided into the various features which are most significant in the normal development of a child; the result, when completed, is a document which points towards areas where change is needed as well as areas where the family experiences particular difficulties.

A further method of assessing family functioning is that of the Hospital for Sick Children, Great Ormond Street, London, which has developed family health scales. These use the concept of a continuum, ranging from breakdown of functioning at one extreme to optimal functioning at the other. In between these two points there will be various levels of care which will include dysfunctional families and those offering adequate care. The context in which the assessment is made is that the family should ideally provide:

1. physical and emotional nurturance of both adults and children

2. socialisation of children

3. maintenance of the emotional health and stability of all family members.

The assessment of a family's functioning is often made as a result of a crisis or breakdown and consequent need to intervene. A one-off serious physical assault, although significant by its nature, should not necessarily be considered to have such a poor prognosis in long-term treatment as the experience of a prolonged period of neglect, both physical and emotional. Regrettably, the latter is more likely to go undetected by professionals until such time as it presents itself in a more acute form and workers may be presented with superficially similar instances of family breakdown, ie physical trauma to a child.

As intervention is often initially based upon a single incident which will become the focus, what we must recognise is that this incident will be in the context of a very significant family pattern. To understand the crisis, it is essential that the nature of the family, subcultural context, and the background to the breakdown be established. If we identify those families whom Polansky talked of as a threat to unprepared or inexperienced workers, then we can accordingly intervene in an appropriate manner, meeting the special needs of the child members of that family and anticipating the pathological resistance.

Treatment approaches

Child care workers use a variety of techniques, sometimes dependent on a philosophy of work, sometimes intuitive responses to the clients involved and, from time to time, within the structured framework of a particular social work methodology or model.

Whatever the context the worker uses he should constantly be aware of the effect he has as an individual on the client family and their position in the community. A willingness to nurture and be supportive may well be effective with some clients. However, this approach may fail dismally with others who require more direction and authority. In some instances too authoritative an approach may undermine the marginally adequate family who allow themselves to be taken over and welcome the respite from responsibility. Unfortunately, it is often by trial and error that the appropriate style is found for a particular family.

Other families need to be directly confronted with the unacceptable level of care they are providing, in order for them to change. They may well need constant and repeated prompting and the child care worker at times needs to be coercive in approach. Goldstein, Freud and Solnit referred to the concept 'fair warning', the need to communicate what is expected of their care to families in order that they may in turn be likely to achieve this. Failure to communicate this to clients may result in moral dilemmas concerning the management of some cases, as the subsequent removal of children will not be seen as consequential upon the failure of parents to respond to specific warnings. Case management will be determined by belated assessment, like 'Is the client likely to cooperate with workers and achieve the required changes?' Such conclusions appear to take years in emerging in the case of many children in care and for others may never be reached.

Making decisions in case management

When we become involved in families which are dysfunctional at the point of crisis or trauma to a child, we may have no alternative to admitting that child into care.

It is, however, possible that if clearer understanding of the family was reached this could indicate how to proceed with the management and enable a speedy return of the child. At times, some children may be apart from their families unnecessarily because of professional anxieties due to our unclear perception of the risks involved in returning them.

Professional response needs to change in order to avoid this danger. If a normally adequate family suffers acute breakdown, appropriate help should aim to re-establish the family and to help them cope once more. Child care workers would expect to be involved for a relatively short time at the end of which the whole family will have re-established autonomy. (See case example 1.)

However, the chronically dysfunctional family in a new crisis will certainly need professional intervention and with these families decisions must be made as to the nature and degree of dysfunction and whether it is tolerable for children to remain with it. If a family is assessed as unable to care for its children then these children should be permanently removed. (See case example 2.) If it is felt that the family is viable then work with this family may need to be either directive or coercive. Another implication in the decision to work with dysfunctional families may be a prolonged commitment to that involvement. Tonge, James and Hillman talked of 'specially prepared workers' to cope with this client group and certainly a distinct response by the worker is necessary for confusion and uncertainty to be avoided in the management of this category of cases. These cases may need continued support until children are less vulnerable by reason of age. Supplementary experiences of school, youth groups and voluntary home visiting will be useful resources to draw upon. (See case example 3.)

Finally, intervention into family life should carry with it a responsibility to ensure satisfactory alternative provision for displaced children and this involves decision-making. It is important that early decisions be made in the context of the greatest possible understanding of family characteristics and their implication for outcome. It would appear that the most sensitive of interventions, if it involves removal of a child, is likely to result in some hurt to that child. In crisis, it is not always feasible to consider 'the least detrimental alternative'. It is however, totally feasible to regard the point at which a child is removed as the commencement of a decision process and not the conclusion of a child-protective intervention. Work is only concluded when the child is returned to the family and they are once again able to offer adequate care, or when the child is placed in a satisfactory substitute placement which offers security and appropriate care.

Case example 1

Family 'A' referred themselves for help to an NSPCC treatment unit. They explained that they were having difficulty controlling their three and a half year-old son and that harsh discipline had been the cause of a recent injury for which hospital treatment had been necessary. Amongst their strategies for controlling their son were locking him in a small cupboard, sticking elastoplast over his mouth to stop screaming and beating with a stick. They were aware that their actions were inappropriate and had recognised this forcibly when the latest incident had resulted in a fracture to his leg.

Enquiries drew out the following information. This was mother's second marriage, unlike her husband's. She was not British and had met her first husband while he was serving with the British Army in

Europe. It had been a violent marriage and her first pregnancy had resulted in a stillbirth following a fight with her husband, who had kicked her in the stomach. Her son had been born following a move to Britain. However, she had subsequently separated from her husband during her third pregnancy because of continued violence, and returned to her parents in Europe. She had met her second husband shortly after this and they had decided to live together. They later returned to Britain where they were married and the second child, a girl, was born. The stepfather had assumed full responsibility for the children, treating them as his own. At the time of referral, mother was still only 22 years of age. Both were considered immature and acknowledged having been indulged by their parents during their respective upbringings.

The family readily agreed to becoming involved in a programme of work which lasted for eight months. During this period mother attended the unit three days a week with both children and was helped to learn more about child development and management techniques. Her particular needs were for consistency and firmness. Additionally, the experience helped mother to learn more of the British culture and to regain her confidence.

Stepfather was involved in the programme once every two or three weeks, as his employment would not permit more frequent attendance. He was also involved in regular reviews together with a social worker from the social services department, who began home visiting and assumed the role of key worker: this continued for some time after the family left the unit.

Multi-disciplinary assessment had no doubt concerning the improvement in the children's development and the reduced risk of physical injury. Additionally, the couple were able to establish a far more mature relationship during this time.

All social work support was withdrawn six months after leaving the unit.

Key factors in assessment
- mother's reaction to broken marriage and stillborn child
- parents' youthfulness and immaturity
- ignorance of child development or management
- social isolation of mother
- no abnormality of parental psycho-pathology

Case example 2

Concern was first expressed about Family 'B' in the maternity unit when this child's mother was seen to smack him; subsequent follow-up was provided in out-patients but mother only kept two appointments.

When the child was five months old, professional concern was mounting and efforts were being made to see the child again. At this point he was presented at the clinic with bruising to the temples and subsequently admitted to hospital. No explanation was offered by mother as to the cause of injuries. She would only say the child was a difficult feeder.

A social worker became involved in the subsequent investigation when it was concluded that this was non-accidental injury. The family was referred to the unit for treatment following a case conference. A decision had been made to offer voluntary care for the child and this was accepted by the parents. If it had not been accepted, care proceedings would have been implemented.

Our assessment considered the prognosis to be poor but help was offered. The mother, aged 23 years and of frail build, was of low intelligence and had received a very sheltered upbringing until the time of her marriage, when she had not only left home but also moved a considerable distance from her family. Her husband had had a breakdown seven years previously when he had been compelled to leave home at the age of 21 years. He had had a difficult adolescence and had spent a year in a psychiatric hostel following a short hospital admission.

It would appear that this couple's marriage had been encouraged by the mother's parents as a way of releasing themselves from the burden of responsibility for her care. The evident difficulties experienced by this couple were perhaps characterised by an incident soon after their marriage when they presented at the local psychiatric hospital and the husband asked that something could be done to alter his wife, to whom he could not relate. They refused, however, to cooperate with marital counselling which was offered.

Work was undertaken with this couple for six months. Initially the mother would attend, collecting the child from foster care, three days each week. Father would attend for part of a day each week. In addition to teaching basic child care skills some marital work was tackled.

Only subsequent to the child's return home did we become fully aware of the nature of this family's dynamics. Father was able to offer little support to his wife, both because of his limitations and her obsessional personality. Under additional stress, mother's fastidiousness over food took on the more sinister appearance of anorexia and she was seen to be withholding food from her son also. Father, when confronted, seemed unable to take any part in protecting his son and both parents became withdrawn.

Care proceedings were taken in this case and the child was returned to the foster parents who had earlier cared for him and who had expressed an interest in adoption in due course. Neither parent opposed this decision when it was made but rather used social work support to look at their continuing personal needs. Eventually the couple split up and the mother returned to her parents' home.

Key factors in assessment
- parental psycho-pathology
- failure to provide care in closely monitored reintroduction of child, ie developmental tests and weekly height/weight measurements
- observation of mother's interaction with son.

Case example 3

Family 'C', a mother and her three children, spent 12 months with us. This was the longest period any family has spent in treatment and it is true to say that we learned from her as well as she from us.

This young woman would absorb all manner of nurture and support but only effectively responded to confrontation and coercion.

At the point at which the family was referred, the mother was isolating herself and neglecting her children. Further, she was failing to respond to the attempts of her social worker or her parents to motivate her to change.

The mother was 27 years old when she came for interview; she looked younger and was surprisingly relaxed. She had three children and her divorce had recently been finalised. Married at 21 years of age, her husband left her several times, the first occasion when the eldest child was 15 months old and the final time when the youngest was six weeks old. In fact he was seldom around when she needed his support and help. She explained that the reason for the breakdown was his association with other women but also referred to his demands for her to 'change' (which she could not explain).

The reason this mother was seeking help was that she believed the three children, six years old, three and a half years old and 18 months old, were beyond control. She also acknowledged her loneliness and the difficulties that the chronic withdrawal from the community had meant for her and the children. She could agree that the house was in a state of squalor and not really fit to bring up a family of young children. The extended family was involved in the contract of work and willingly helped in the task of redecorating the home. However, they also made it clear that they would not assume responsibility for this young woman.

The initial contract stipulated a six month period of attendance, three days each week, and this was honoured. However, as the end neared there was a deterioration. With renewed effort all would go well until again we would suggest that it was time to conclude treatment in the day centre: then there would be a deterioration. We appeared to have fallen into a dependency trap.

What we initially failed to recognise was that this woman responded to confrontation. Attempts to leave her with a sense of achievement and increased self-esteem failed as she responded only to authoritative instructions. She appeared not to function totally independently. Therefore ultimata were issued and these invariably gained a response: for example, the house must be cleaned, the children must get to school on time.

The community social worker, together with a family aide, worked closely with us and eventually a pattern of weekly visiting was established to monitor the standards in this home and to challenge mother if they faltered. In this way an adequate environment has been established for the children, supplemented by schooling.

There was never doubt that this mother loved her children. Our concern was about the level of care provided and it may well need a continued input of resources to enable adequate care to be maintained. However, we feel this to be appropriate for these three children.

Key factors in assessment
- inappropriate attitude to problems, ie failure to be concerned about bad home situation
- emotional immaturity despite life experience
- undoing of practical help, disregard of any material possessions
- dissociation with parental responsibility, appearing to ignore the needs of children whilst apparently loving them
- leaving the workers with anxieties about the children whilst appearing carefree.

References

Goldstein J, Freud A and Solnit A
(1973) *Beyond the best interests of the child.* Free Press.

Goldstein J, Freud A and Solnit A
(1980) *Before the best interests of the child.* Burnett/Deutsch.

Lynch M A and Roberts J
(1982) *Consequences of child abuse.* Academic Press.

Polansky N A, Borgman and De Soux
(1972) *The roots of futility.* Jossey-Bass.

Polansky N A, Chalmers M A, Buttenwieser E and Williams D P
(1981) *Damaged parents: an anatomy of neglect.* Chicago: University
of Chicago Press.

Pringle M K
(1975) *The needs of children.* Hutchinson Educational Ltd.

Tonge W L, James D S and Hillman S
(1975) 'Families without hope'. *British Journal of Psychiatry* Special
Publication.

Checklists

Vera Fahlberg

Dr Vera Fahlberg, a psychotherapist with a paediatric background, is Medical Director of Forest Heights Lodge, Colorado, USA, a psychiatric treatment centre for emotionally disturbed boys.

Observation checklist: What to look for in assessing attachment

1. Birth to one year

Does the child...?
- appear alert?
- respond to humans?
- show interest in the human face?
- track with his eyes?
- vocalise frequently?
- exhibit expected motor development?
- enjoy close physical contact?
- exhibit discomfort?
- appear to be easily comforted?
- exhibit normal or excessive fussiness?
- appear outgoing or is he passive and withdrawn?
- have good muscle tone?
- others:

Does the parent(s)...?
- respond to the infant's vocalisations?
- change voice tone when talking to the infant or about the infant?
- show interest in face to face contact with the infant?
- exhibit interest in and encourage age-appropriate development?
- respond to the child's indications of discomfort?
- show the ability to comfort the child?
- enjoy close physical contact with the child?
- initiate positive interactions with the child?
- identify positive or negative qualities in the child that remind the parent of another family member?
- others:

2. One to five years

Does the child...?
- explore the environment in a normal way?
- respond to parent(s)?
- keep himself occupied in a positive way?
- seem relaxed and happy?

- have the ability to express emotions?
- react to pain and pleasure?
- engage in age-appropriate activity?
- use speech appropriately?
- express frustration?
- respond to parental limit setting?
- exhibit observable fears?
- react positively to physical closeness?
- respond appropriately to separation from parent?
- respond appropriately to parent's return?
- exhibit body rigidity or relaxation?
- others:

Does the parent(s)...?
- use appropriate disciplinary measures?
- show interest in child's development?
- respond to child's overtures?
- encourage physical closeness with the child?
- comfort the child in positive way?
- initiate positive interactions with the child?
- accept expressions of autonomy?
- see the child as 'taking after' someone? Is this positive or negative?
- others:

3. Primary school children

Does the child...?
- behave as though he likes himself?
- appear proud of accomplishments?
- share?
- perform well academically?
- always test limits?
- try new tasks?
- react realistically to making a mistake? Does he show fear, anger or acceptance?
- have the ability to express emotions?
- establish eye contact?
- exhibit confidence in his abilities or does he frequently say 'I don't know'?
- appear to be developing a conscience?
- move in a relaxed way or is there body rigidity?
- feel comfortable speaking to adults?
- smile easily?
- react to parent(s) being physically close?
- have positive interactions with siblings and/or peers?
- appear comfortable with his sexual identification?
- others:

Does the parent(s)...?
- show interest in child's school performance?

- accept expression of negative feelings?
- respond to child's overtures?
- give support for child in terms of developing healthy peer relationships?
- handle problems between siblings equitably?
- initiate affectionate overtures?
- use appropriate disciplinary measures?
- assign age-appropriate responsibilities to the child?
- others:

4. Adolescents

Is the adolescent...?
- aware of his strong points?
- aware of his weak points?
- comfortable with his sexuality?
- engaging in positive peer interactions?
- performing satisfactorily in school?
- exhibiting signs of conscience development?
- free from severe problems with the law?
- accepting and/or rejecting parents' value system?
- keeping himself occupied in appropriate ways?
- comfortable with reasonable limits or is he constantly involved in control issues?
- developing interests outside the home?
- others:

Does the parent(s)...?
- set appropriate limits?
- encourage appropriate autonomy?
- trust the adolescent?
- show interest in and acceptance of adolescent's friends?
- display interest in adolescent's school performance?
- exhibit interest in adolescent's outside activities?
- have reasonable expectations of chores and/or responsibilities adolescent should assume?
- stand by the adolescent if he gets into trouble?
- show affection?
- think this child will 'turn out' okay?
- others:

Observation checklist: Long-range effects of lack of normal attachment

Psychological or behavioural problems

Conscience development
- May not show normal anxiety following aggressive or cruel behaviour.

- May not show guilt on breaking laws or rules.
- May project blame on others.

Impulse control
- Exhibits poor control; depends upon others to provide external controls on behaviour.
- Exhibits lack of foresight.
- Has a poor attention span.

Self-esteem
- Is unable to get satisfaction from tasks well done.
- Sees self as undeserving.
- Sees self as incapable of change.
- Has difficulty having fun.

Interpersonal interactions
- Lacks trust in others.
- Demands affection but lacks depth in relationships.
- Exhibits hostile dependency.
- Needs to be in control of all situations.
- Has impaired social maturity.

Emotions
- Has trouble recognising own feelings.
- Has difficulty expressing feelings appropriately; especially anger, sadness and frustration.
- Has difficulty recognising feelings in others.

Cognitive problems
- Has trouble with basic cause and effect.
- Experiences problems with logical thinking.
- Appears to have confused thought processes.
- Has difficulty thinking ahead.
- May have an impaired sense of time.
- Has difficulties with abstract thinking.

Developmental problems
- May have difficulty with auditory processing.
- May have difficulty expressing self well verbally.
- May have gross motor problems.
- May experience delays in fine-motor adaptive skills.
- May experience delays in personal-social development.
- May have inconsistent levels of skills in all of the above areas.

Checklist: Ways to encourage attachment

Responding to the arousal/relaxation cycle
- Using the child's tantrums to encourage attachment.

- Responding to the child when he is physically ill.
- Accompanying the child to doctor and dentist appointments.
- Helping the child express and cope with feelings of anger and frustration.
- Sharing the child's extreme excitement over his achievements.
- Helping the child cope with feelings about moving.
- Helping the child cope with ambivalent feelings about his birth family.
- Helping the child learn more about his past.
- Responding to a child who is hurt or injured.
- Educating the child about sexual issues.
- Others:

Initiating positive interactions

- Making affectionate overtures: hugs, kisses, physical closeness.
- Reading to the child.
- Sharing the child's 'life book'.
- Playing games.
- Going shopping together for clothes/toys for child.
- Going on special outings: circus, plays, or the like.
- Supporting the child's outside activities by providing transport or being a group leader.
- Helping the child with homework when he or she needs it.
- Teaching the child to cook or bake.
- Saying 'I love you'.
- Teaching the child about extended family members through pictures and talk.
- Helping the child understand the family 'jokes' or sayings.
- Teaching the child to participate in family activities such as bowling, camping, or ski-ing.
- Helping the child meet expectations of the other parent.
- Others:

Encouraging behaviour

- Encouraging the child to practise calling parents 'mum' and 'dad'.
- Adding a *middle* name to incorporate a name of family significance.
- Hanging pictures of child on wall.
- Involving the child in family reunions and similar activities.
- Involving the child in grandparent visits.
- Including the child in family rituals.
- Holding religious ceremonies or other ceremonies that incorporate the child into the family.
- Buying new clothes for the child as a way of becoming acquainted with child's size, colour preferences, style preferences, and the like.
- Making statements such as 'in our family do it this way' in supportive fashion.
- Sending out announcements of adoption.
- Others:

Chart illustrating the developmental progress of infants and young children

Mary Sheridan

Age	Posture and large movements	Vision and fine movements
1 MONTH	Lies back with head to one side; arm and leg on same side outstretched, or both arms flexed; knees apart, soles of feet turned inwards. Large jerky movements of limbs, arms more active than legs. At rest, hands closed and thumb turned in. Fingers and toes fan out during extensor movements of limbs. When cheek touched, turns to same side; ear gently rubbed, turns head away. When lifted or pulled to sit head falls loosely backwards. Held sitting, head falls forward, with back in one complete curve. Placed downwards on face, head immediately turns to side; arms and legs flexed under body, buttocks humped up. Held standing on hard surface, presses down feet, straightens body and often makes reflex 'stepping' movements.	Turns head and eyes towards light. Stares expressionlessly at brightness of window or blank wall. Follows pencil flash-lamp briefly with eyes at 1 foot. Shuts eyes tightly when pencil light shone directly into them at 1-2 inches. Notices silent dangling toy shaken in line of vision at 6-8 inches and follows its slow movement with eyes from side towards mid-line on level with face through approximately quarter circle, before head falls back to side. Gazes at mother's nearby face when she feeds or talks to him with increasingly alert facial expression.
3 MONTHS	Now prefers to lie on back with head in mid-line. Limbs more pliable, movements smoother and more continuous. Waves arms symmetrically. Hands now loosely open. Brings hands together from side into mid-line over chest or chin. Kicks vigorously, legs alternating or occasionally together. Held sitting, holds back straight, except in lumbar region, with head erect and steady for several seconds before bobbing forwards. Placed downwards on face lifts head and upper chest well up in mid-line, using forearms as support, and often scratching at table surface; legs straight, buttocks flat. Held standing with feet on hard surface, sags at knees.	Visually very alert, particularly interested in nearby human faces. Moves head deliberately to look around him. Follows adult's movements near cot. Follows dangling toy at 6-10 inches above face through half circle from side to side, and usually also vertically from chest to brow. Watches movements of own hands before face and beginning to clasp and unclasp hands together in finger play. Recognises feeding bottle and makes eager welcoming movements as it approaches his face. Regards still objects within 6-10 inches for more than a second or two, but seldom fixates continuously. Comerges eyes as dangling toy is moved towards face. Defensive blink shown.

We are grateful to Her Majesty's Stationery Office for permission to publish this chart, which has been extracted from Reports on Public Health and Medical Subjects *No 102. Dr Sheridan designed the chart in 1960 and it was revised in 1975. It is still considered by many leading paediatricians to be one of the most reliable descriptions of normal human development in the early years.*

Hearing and speech

Startled by sudden loud noises, stiffens, quivers, blinks, screws eyes up, extends limbs, fans out fingers and toes, and may cry.

Movements momentarily 'frozen', when small bell rung gently 3–5 inches from ear for 3–5 seconds, with 5 second pauses: may 'corner' eyes towards sound.

Stops whimpering to sound of nearby soothing human voice, but not when screaming or feeding.

Cries lustily when hungry or uncomfortable.

Utters little guttural noises when content.

(*Note.* – Deaf babies also cry and vocalise in this reflex way, but if very deaf do not usually show startle reflex to sudden noise. Blind babies may also move eyes towards a sound-making toy. Vision should always be checked separately.)

Social behaviour and play

Sucks well.

Sleeps much of the time when not being fed or handled.

Expression still vague, but becoming more alert, progressing to social smiling about 5–6 weeks.

Hands normally closed, but if opened, grasps examiner's finger when palm is touched.

Stops crying when picked up and spoken to.

Mother supports head when carrying, dressing and bathing.

Sudden loud noises still distress, provoking blinking, screwing up of eyes, crying and turning away.

Definite quietening or smiling to sound of mother's voice before she touches him, but not when screaming.

Vocalises freely when spoken to or pleased.

Cries when uncomfortable or annoyed.

Quietens to tinkle of spoon in cup or to bell rung gently out of sight for 3–5 seconds at 6–12 inches from ear. May turn eyes and head towards sound: brows may wrinkle and eyes dilate.

Often licks lips in response to sounds of preparation for feeding.

Shows excitement at sound of approaching footsteps, running bath water, voices, etc.

(*Note.* – Deaf baby, instead, may be obviously startled by mother's sudden appearance beside cot.)

Fixes eyes unblinkingly on mother's face when feeding.

Beginning to react to familiar situations – showing by smiles, coos, and excited movements that he recognises preparation for feeds, baths, etc.

Responds with obvious pleasure to friendly handling, especially when accompanied by playful tickling and vocal sounds.

Holds rattle for few moments when placed in hand, but seldom capable of regarding it at same time.

Mother supports at shoulders when dressing and bathing.

Age	Posture and large movements	Vision and fine movements
6 MONTHS	Lying on back, raises head from pillow. Lifts legs into vertical and grasps foot. Sits with support in cot or pram and turns head from side to side to look around him. Moves arms in brisk and purposeful fashion and holds them up to be lifted. When hands grasped braces shoulders and pulls himself up. Kicks strongly, legs alternating. Can roll over, front to back. Held sitting, head is firmly erect, and back straight. May sit alone momentarily. Placed downwards on face lifts head and chest well up, supporting himself on extended arms. Held standing with feet touching hard surface bears weight on feet and bounces up and down actively.	Visually insatiable: moves head and eyes eagerly in every direction. Eyes move in unison: squint now abnormal. Follows adult's movements across room. Immediately fixates interesting small objects within 6-12 inches (eg, toy, bell, wooden cube, spoon, sweet) and stretches out both hands to grasp them. Uses whole hand in palmar grasp. When toys fall from hand over edge of cot forgets them. (Watches rolling balls of 2 to ¼ inch diameter at 10 feet.)
9 MONTHS	Sits alone for 10-15 minutes on floor. Can turn body to look sideways while stretching out to grasp dangling toy or to pick up toy from floor. Arms and legs very active in cot, pram and bath. Progresses on floor by rolling or squirming. Attempts to crawl on all fours. Pulls self to stand with support. Can stand holding on to support for a few moments, but cannot lower himself. Held standing, steps purposefully on alternate feet.	Very observant. Stretches out, one hand leading, to grasp small objects immediately on catching sight of them. Manipulates objects with lively interest, passing from hand to hand, turning over, etc. Pokes at small sweet with index finger. Grasps sweets, string, etc., between finger and thumb in scissor fashion. Can release toy by pressing against firm surface, but cannot yet put down precisely. Searches in correct place for toys dropped within reach of hands. Looks after toys falling over edge of pram or table. Watches activities of adults, children and animals within 10-12 feet with eager interest for several seconds at a time. (Watches rolling balls 2 − ⅛ inches at 10 feet.)

Hearing and speech

Turns immediately to mother's voice across room.
Vocalises tunefully and often, using single and double syllables, eg, ka, muh, goo, der, adah, er-leh.
Laughs, chuckles and squeals aloud in play.
Screams with annoyance.
Shows evidence of response to different emotional tones of mother's voice.
Responds to baby hearing tests at 1½ feet from each ear by correct visual localisation, but may show slightly brisker response on one side. (Tests employed – voice, rattle, cup and spoons, paper, bell; 2 seconds with 2 seconds pause.)

Social behaviour and play

Hands competent to reach for and grasp small toys. Most often uses a two-handed, scooping-in approach, but occasionally a single hand.
Takes everything to mouth.
Beginning to find feet interesting and even useful in grasping.
Puts hands to bottle and pats it when feeding.
Shakes rattle deliberately to make it sound, often regarding it closely at same time.
Still friendly with strangers but occasionally shows some shyness or even slight anxiety, especially if mother is out of sight.

Vocalises deliberately as means of interpersonal communication.
Shouts to attract attention, listens, then shouts again.
Babbles tunefully, repeating syllables in long strings (mam-mam, bab-bab, dad-dad, etc.)
Understands 'No-No' and 'Bye-Bye'.
Tries to imitate adults' playful vocal sounds, eg smacking lips, cough, brr, etc.
(Immediate localising response to baby hearing tests at 3 feet from ear and above and below ear level.)

Holds, bites and chews biscuits.
Puts hands round bottle or cup when feeding.
Tries to grasp spoon when being fed.
Throws body back and stiffens in annoyance or resistance.
Clearly distinguishes strangers from familiars, and requires reassurance before accepting their advances.
Clings to known adult and hides face.
Still takes everything to mouth.
Seizes bell in one hand. Imitates ringing action, waving or banging it on table, pokes clapper or 'drinks' from bowl.
Plays peek-a-boo.
Holds out toy held in hand to adult, but cannot yet give.
Finds partially hidden toy.
May find toy hidden under cup.
Mother supports at lower spine when dressing.

Age	Posture and large movements	Vision and fine movements
12 MONTHS	Sits well and for indefinite time. Can rise to sitting position from lying down. Crawls rapidly, usually on all fours. Pulls to standing and lets himself down again holding on to furniture. Walks round furniture stepping sideways. Walks with one or both hands held. May stand alone for few moments. May walk alone.	Picks up small objects, eg blocks, string, sweets and crumbs, with precise pincer grasp of thumb and index finger. Throws toys deliberately and watches them fall to ground. Looks in correct place for toys which roll out of sight. Points with index finger at objects he wants to handle or which interest him. Watches small toy pulled along floor across room 10 feet away. Out of doors watches movements of people, animals, motor cars, etc., with prolonged intent regard. Recognises familiars approaching from 20 feet or more away. Uses both hands freely, but may show preference for one. Clicks two bricks together in imitation. (Watches rolling balls $2 - \frac{1}{8}$ inches at 10 feet.)
15 MONTHS	Walks unevenly with feet wide apart, arms slightly flexed and held above head or at shoulder level to balance. Starts alone, but frequently stopped by falling or bumping into furniture. Lets himself down from standing to sitting by collapsing backwards with bump, or occasionally by falling forward on hands and then back to sitting. Can get to feet alone. Crawls upstairs. Kneels unaided or with slight support on floor and in pram, cot and bath. May be able to stoop to pick up toys from floor.	Picks up string, small sweets and crumbs neatly between thumb and finger. Builds tower of two cubes after demonstration. Grasps crayon and imitates scribble after demonstration. Looks with interest at pictures in book and pats page. Follows with eyes path of cube or small toy swept vigorously from table. Watches small toy pulled across floor up to 12 feet. Points imperiously to objects he wishes to be given. Stands at window and watches events outside intently for several minutes. (Watches and retrieves rolling balls of $2 - \frac{1}{8}$ inches at 10 feet.)

Hearing and speech

Knows and immediately turns to own name.
Babbles loudly, tunefully and incessantly.
Shows by suitable movements and behaviour that he understands several words in usual context (eg own and family names, walk, dinner, pussy, cup, spoon, ball, car).
Comprehends simple commands associated with gesture (give it to daddy, come to mummy, say bye-bye, clap hands, etc.).
Imitates adults' playful vocalisations with gleeful enthusiasm.
May hand examiner common objects on request, eg spoon, cup, ball, shoe.
(Immediate response to baby tests at 3–4½ feet but rapidly habituates.)

Social behaviour and play

Drinks from cup with little assistance. Chews.
Holds spoon but usually cannot use it alone.
Helps with dressing by holding out arm for sleeve and foot for shoe.
Takes objects to mouth less often.
Puts wooden cubes in and out of cup or box.
Rattles spoon in cup in imitation.
Seizes bell by handle and rings briskly in imitation, etc.
Listens with obvious pleasure to percussion sounds.
Repeats activities to reproduce effects.
Gives toys to adult on request and sometimes spontaneously. Finds hidden toy quickly.
Likes to be constantly within sight and hearing of adult.
Demonstrates affection to familiars.
Waves 'bye-bye' and claps hands in imitation or spontaneously.
Child sits, or sometimes stands without support, while mother dresses.

Jabbers loudly and freely, using wide range of inflections and phonetic units.
Speaks 2–6 recognisable words and understands many more.
Vocalises wishes and needs at table.
Points to familiar persons, animals, toys, etc. when requested.
Understands and obeys simple commands (eg shut the door, give me the ball, get your shoes).
(Baby test 4½-6 feet.)

Holds cup when adult gives and takes back.
Holds spoon, brings it to mouth and licks it, but cannot prevent its turning over. Chews well.
Helps more constructively with dressing.
Indicates when he has wet pants.
Pushes large wheeled toy with handle on level ground.
Seldom takes toys to mouth.
Repeatedly casts objects to floor in play or rejection, usually without watching fall.
Physically restless and intensely curious.
Handles everything within reach.
Emotionally labile.
Closely dependent upon adult's reassuring presence.
Needs constant supervision to protect child from dangers of extended exploration and exploitation of environment.

101

Age	Posture and large movements	Vision and fine movements
18 MONTHS	Walks well with feet only slightly apart, starts and stops safely. Runs stiffly upright, eyes fixed on ground 1-2 yards ahead, but cannot continue to run round obstacles. Pushes and pulls large toys, boxes, etc., round floor. Can carry large doll or teddy-bear while walking and sometimes two. Backs into small chair or slides in sideways. Climbs forward into adult's chair then turns round and sits. Walks upstairs with helping hand. Creeps backwards downstairs. Occasionally bumps down a few steps on buttocks facing forwards. Picks up toy from floor without falling.	Picks up small sweets, beads, pins, threads, etc., immediately on sight, with delicate pincer grasp. Spontaneous scribble when given crayon and paper, using preferred hand. Builds tower of three cubes after demonstration. Enjoys simple picture book, often recognising and putting finger on coloured items on page. Turns pages 2 or 3 at a time. Fixes eyes on small dangling toy up to 10 feet. (May tolerate this test with each eye separately.) Points to distant interesting objects out of doors. (Watches and retrieves rolling balls 2—⅛ inches at 10 feet.) (Possibly recognises special miniature toys at 10 feet.)
2 YEARS	Runs safely on whole foot, stopping and starting with ease and avoiding obstacles. Squats to rest or to play with object on ground and rises to feet without using hands. Walks backwards pulling large toy. Pulls wheeled toy by cord. Climbs on furniture to look out of window or open doors, etc., and can get down again. Walks upstairs and down holding on to rail or wall: two feet to a step. Throws small ball without falling. Walks into large ball when trying to kick it. Sits astride large wheeled toy and propels forward with feet on ground.	Picks up pins and thread, etc., neatly and quickly. Removes paper wrapping from small sweet. Builds tower of six cubes (or 6 +). Spontaneous circular scribble and dots when given paper and pencil. Imitates vertical line (and sometimes V). Enjoys picture books, recognising fine details in favourite pictures. Turns pages singly. Recognises familiar adults in photograph after once shown. Hand preference becoming evident. (Immediately catches sight of, and names special miniature toys at 10 feet distance. Will now usually tolerate this test with each eye separately.) (Watches and retrieves rolling balls 2−⅛ inches at 10 feet.)

Hearing and speech	Social behaviour and play
Continues to jabber tunefully to himself at play. Uses 6–20 recognisable words and understands many more. Echoes prominent or last word addressed to him. Demands desired objects by pointing accompanied by loud, urgent vocalisation or single words. Enjoys nursery rhymes and tries to join in. Attempts to sing. Shows his own or doll's hair, shoe, nose. (Possibly special 5 toy test. Possibly 4 animals picture test.)	Lifts and holds cup between both hands. Drinks without spilling. Hands cup back to adult. Chews well. Holds spoon and gets food to mouth. Takes off shoes, socks, hat. Indicates toilet needs by restlessness and vocalisation. Bowel control usually attained. Explores environment energetically. No longer takes toys to mouth. Remembers where objects belong. Casts objects to floor in play or anger less often. Briefly imitates simple activities, eg reading book, kissing doll, brushing floor. Plays contentedly alone, but likes to be near adult. Emotionally still very dependent upon familiar adult, especially mother. Alternates between clinging and resistance.
Uses 50 or more recognisable words and understands many more. Puts 2 or more words together to form simple sentences. Refers to himself by name. Talks to himself continually as he plays. Echolalia almost constant, with one or more stressed words repeated. Constantly asking names of objects. Joins in nursery rhymes and songs. Shows correctly and repeats words for hair, hand, feet, nose, eyes, mouth, shoe on request. (6 toy test, 4 animals picture test.)	Lifts and drinks from cup and replaces on table. Spoon-feeds without spilling. Asks for food and drink. Chews competently. Puts on hat and shoes. Verbalises toilet needs in reasonable time. Dry during day. Turns door handles. Often runs outside to explore. Follows mother round house and copies domestic activities in simultaneous play. Engages in simple make-believe activities. Constantly demanding mother's attention. Clings tightly in affection, fatigue or fear. Tantrums when frustrated but attention readily distracted. Defends own possessions with determination. As yet no idea of sharing. Plays near other children but not with them. Resentful of attention shown to other children.

Age	Posture and large movements	Vision and fine movements
2½ YEARS	Walks upstairs alone but downstairs holding rail, two feet to a step. Runs well straight forward and climbs easy nursery apparatus. Pushes and pulls large toys skilfully, but has difficulty in steering them round obstacles. Jumps with two feet together. Can stand on tiptoe if shown. Kicks large ball. Sits on tricycle and steers with hands, but still usually propels with feet on ground.	Picks up pins, threads, etc., with each eye covered separately. Builds tower of seven (or 7+) cubes and lines blocks to form 'train'. Recognises minute details in picture books. Imitates horizontal line and circle (also usually T and V). Paints strokes, dots and circular shapes on easel. Recognises himself in photographs when once shown. Recognises miniature toys and retrieves balls 2 – ⅛ inches at 10 feet, each eye separately. (May also match special single letter-cards V, O, T, H at 10 feet.)
3 YEARS	Walks alone upstairs with alternating feet and downstairs with two feet to step. Usually jumps from bottom step. Climbs nursery apparatus with agility. Can turn round obstacles and corners while running and also while pushing and pulling large toys. Rides tricycle and can turn wide corners on it. Can walk on tiptoe. Stands momentarily on one foot when shown. Sits with feet crossed at ankles.	Picks up pins, threads, etc, with each eye covered separately. Builds tower of nine cubes, also (3½) bridge of three from model. Can close fist and wiggle thumb in imitation. R and L. Copies circle (also V, H, T). Imitates cross. Draws man with head and usually indication of features or one other part. Matches two or three primary colours (usually red and yellow correct, but may confuse blue and green). Paints 'pictures' with large brush on easel. Cuts with scissors. (Recognises special miniature toys at 10 feet. Performs single-letter vision test at 10 feet. Five letters.)

Hearing and speech

Uses 200 or more recognisable words but speech shows numerous infantilisms.
Knows full name.
Talks intelligibly to himself at play concerning events happening here and now.
Echolalia persists.
Continually asking questions beginning 'What?', 'Where?'.
Uses pronouns, I, me and you.
Stuttering in eagerness common.
Says a few nursery rhymes.
Enjoys simple familiar stories read from picture book.
(6 toy test, 4 animals picture test, 1st cube test. Full doll vocabulary.)

Social behaviour and play

Eats skilfully with spoon and may use fork.
Pulls down pants or knickers at toilet, but seldom able to replace.
Dry through night if lifted.
Very active, restless and rebellious.
Throws violent tantrums when thwarted or unable to express urgent needs and less easily distracted.
Emotionally still very dependent upon adults.
Prolonged domestic make-believe play (putting dolls to bed, washing clothes, driving motor cars, etc.) but with frequent reference to friendly adult.
Watches other children at play interestedly and occasionally joins in for a few minutes, but little notion of sharing playthings or adult's attention.

Large intelligible vocabulary but speech still shows many infantile phonetic substitutions.
Gives full name and sex, and (sometimes) age.
Uses plurals and pronouns.
Still talks to himself in long monologues mostly concerned with the immediate present, including make-believe activities.
Carries on simple conversations, and verbalises past experiences.
Asks many questions beginning 'What?', 'Where?', 'Who?'.
Listens eagerly to stories and demands favourites over and over again.
Knows several nursery rhymes.
(7 toy test, 4 animals picture test. 1st or 2nd cube test, 6 'high frequency' word pictures.)

Eats with fork and spoon.
Washes hands, but needs supervision in drying.
Can pull pants and knickers down and up, but needs help with buttons.
Dry through night.
General behaviour more amenable.
Affectionate and confiding.
Likes to help with adult's activities in house and garden.
Makes effort to keep his surroundings tidy.
Vividly realised make-believe play including invented people and objects.
Enjoys floor play with bricks, boxes, toy trains and cars, alone or with siblings.
Joins in play with other children in and outdoors.
Understands sharing playthings, sweets, etc.
Shows affection for younger siblings.
Shows some appreciation of past and present.

Age	Posture and large movements	Vision and fine movements
4 Y E A R S	Turns sharp corners running, pushing and pulling. Walks alone up and downstairs, one foot per step. Climbs ladders and trees. Can run on tiptoe. Expert rider of tricycle. Hops on one foot. Stands on one foot 3-5 seconds. Arranges or picks up objects from floor by bending from waist with knees extended.	Picks up pins, thread, crumbs, etc., with each eye covered separately. Builds tower of 10 or more cubes and several 'bridges' of three on request. Builds three steps with six cubes after demonstration. Imitates spreading of hand and bringing thumb into opposition with each finger in turn. R and L. Copies cross (also V, H, T, O). Draws man with head, legs, features, trunk, and (often) arms. Draws very simple house. Matches and names four primary colours correctly. (Single-letter vision test at 10 feet, seven letters: also near chart to bottom.)
5 Y E A R S	Runs lightly on toes. Active and skilful in climbing, sliding, swinging, digging and various 'stunts'. Skips on alternate feet. Dances to music. Can stand on one foot 8-10 seconds. Can hop 2-3 yards forwards on each foot separately. Grips strongly with either hand.	Picks up minute objects when each eye is covered separately. Builds three steps with six cubes from model. Copies square and triangle (also letters: V, T, H, O, X, L, A, C, U, Y). Writes a few letters spontaneously. Draws recognisable man with head, trunk, legs, arms and features. Draws simple house with door, windows, roof and chimney. Counts fingers on one hand with index finger of other. Names four primary colours and matches 10 or 12 colours. (Full nine-letter vision chart at 20 feet and near test to bottom.)

Hearing and speech

Speech completely intelligible.
Shows only a few infantile
substitutions usually k/t/th/f/s and
r/l/w/y groups).
Gives connected account of recent
events and experiences.
Gives name, sex, home address and
(usually) age.
Eternally asking questions 'Why?',
'When?', 'How?' and meanings of
words.
Listens to and tells long stories
sometimes confusing fact and
fantasy.
(7 toy test, 1st picture vocabulary
test, 2nd cube test.
6 'high frequency' word pictures.)

Social behaviour and play

Eats skilfully with spoon and fork.
Washes and dries hands. Brushes
teeth.
Can undress and dress except for
back buttons, laces and ties.
General behaviour markedly self-
willed.
Inclined to verbal impertinence
when wishes crossed but can be
affectionate and compliant.
Strongly dramatic play and dressing-
up favoured.
Constructive out-of-doors building
with any large material to hand.
Needs other children to play with
and is alternately co-operative and
aggressive with them as with adults.
Understands taking turns.
Shows concern for younger siblings
and sympathy for playmates in
distress.
Appreciates past, present and future.

Speech fluent and grammatical.
Articulation correct except for
residual confusions of s/f/th and
r/l/w/y groups.
Loves stories and acts them out in
detail later.
Gives full name, age and home
address.
Gives age and (usually) birthday.
Defines concrete nouns by use.
Asks meaning of abstract words.
(12 'high frequency' picture
vocabulary or word lists. 3rd cube
test, 6 sentences.)

Uses knife and fork.
Washes and dries face and hands, but
needs help and supervision for rest.
Undresses and dresses alone.
General behaviour more sensible,
controlled and responsibly
independent.
Domestic and dramatic play
continued from day to day.
Plans and builds constructively.
Floor games very complicated.
Chooses own friends.
Co-operative with companions and
understands need for rules and fair
play.
Appreciates meaning of clocktime in
relation to daily programme.
Tender and protective towards
younger children and pets. Comforts
playmates in distress.

Scales

Norman A Polansky

Norman A Polansky is Regent's Professor of Social Work at the University of Georgia and has worked as a caseworker, psychotherapist and supervisor in private psychiatric hospitals.

The childhood level of living scale and the maternal characteristics scale both appeared in Damaged parents: an anatomy of neglect *by Norman A Polansky, Mary Ann Chalmers, Elizabeth Buttenwieser and David P Williams, Chicago and London: Chicago University Press, 1981.*

Note: *these scales are included as examples of the type of checklist in use in the USA, useful for helping to assess levels of living. They are not, however, intended as models for UK practice and it will be evident that some of the questions are not relevant here.*

Childhood level of living scale

Part A – Physical care

	Key to Scoring	
I General positive child care	**Yes**	**No**
1. Mother plans at least one meal consisting of two courses.	1	
2. Mother uses good judgment about leaving child alone in the house.	1	
3. Mother plans for variety in foods.	1	
4. Mother sometimes leaves child to insufficiently older sibling.		1
5. Mother plans meals with courses that go together.	1	
6. The child receives at least 9 hours of sleep most nights.	1	
7. Child is offered food at fixed time each day.	1	
8. Bedtime for the child is set by the parents for about the same time each night.	1	
9. Mother has evidenced lack of awareness of child's possible dental needs.		1
10. Mother expresses concern about feeding a balanced diet.	1	
11. Mother enforces rules about going into the street.	1	
12. Child has been taught own address.	1	
13. Child is taught to swim or mother believes child should be taught to swim.	1	
14. Mother will never leave child alone in the house.	1	
15. Mother uses thermometer with child.	1	
II State of repair of house		
16. Storm sashes or equivalent are present.	1	
17. Windows are caulked or sealed against draughts.	1	

	Yes	No
18. Doors are weatherproofed.	1	
19. House is dilapidated.		1
20. There are window screens in good repair in most windows.	1	
21. Wood floors are cracked and splintered.		1
22. There are screen doors properly mounted.	1	
23. There is an operating electric sweeper.	1	
24. Floor covering presents tripping hazard.		1
25. Living room doubles as a bedroom.		1

III Negligence (reciprocal meaning)

	Yes	No
26. There are food scraps on the floor and furniture.		1
27. Child 5 years or older sleeps in room with parents.		1
28. At least one of the children sleeps in the same bed as parents.		1
29. Mother plans special meals for special occasions.	1	
30. Windows have been cracked or broken over a month without repair.		1
31. Clothing usually appears to be hand-me-downs.		1
32. Buttons and snaps of child's clothing are frequently missing and not replaced.		1

IV Quality of household maintenance

	Yes	No
33. There are dirty dishes and utensils in rooms other than the kitchen.		1
34. There are leaky faucets.		1
35. The roof (or ceiling) leaks.		1
36. The floors of the house appear to be swept each day.	1	
37. Bathroom seems to be cleaned regularly.	1	
38. Mother takes precautions in the storage of medicine.	1	
39. Mattresses are in obviously poor condition.		1
40. Repairs one usually makes oneself are left undone.		1

V Quality of health care and grooming

	Yes	No
41. Mother has encouraged child to wash hands before meals.	1	
42. Ears are usually clean.	1	
43. Mother mentions she makes effort to get child to eat food not preferred because they are important to child's nutrition.	1	
44. Poisonous or dangerous sprays and cleaning fluids are stored out of child's reach.	1	
45. Mother has encouraged child to wash hands after using toilet.	1	
46. Mother cautions child to be careful of flaking paint.	1	
47. It is obvious that mother has given attention to child's grooming at home.	1	

Part B – Emotional/cognitive care

VI Encouraging competence

	Yes	No
48. Planned overnight vacation trip has been taken by family.	1	
49. Child has been taken by parents to see some well known historical or cultural building.	1	
50. Child has been taken by parents to see a spectator sport.	1	
51. Mother mentions that in the last year she has: taught the child something about nature; told the child a story; read a story to the child.	1	
52. Family has taken child downtown.	1	
53. Child has been taken by parents to see various animals.	1	
54. Child has been taken by parents to a carnival.	1	
55. Mother is tuned into child's indirect emotional signals.	1	
56. Mother mentions that she has played games with the child.	1	
57. Mother mentions use of TV to teach child.	1	
58. Child has been taken by parents to a parade.	1	
59. A prayer is said before some meals.	1	
60. Mother comforts the child when he is upset.	1	
61. There are magazines available.	1	
62. The family owns a camera.	1	
63. The child says prayers at bedtime.	1	
64. Child has been taken to a children's movie.	1	
65. Mother mentions that she answers child's questions about how things work.	1	
66. Child has been taken by parents to the firehouse.	1	
67. Child has been taken fishing.	1	

VII Inconsistency of discipline and coldness (reciprocal meaning)

	Yes	No
68. Mother seems not to follow through on rewards.		1
69. Mother mentions that she cannot get child to mind.		1
70. Child is often ignored when he tries to tell mother something.		1
71. The child is often pushed aside when he shows need for love.		1
72. Mother seems not to follow through on threatened punishments.		1
73. Spanking is sometimes with an object.		1
74. Mother threatens punishment by imagined or real fright object.		1
75. Very frequently no action is taken when discipline is indicated.		1
76. Mother frequently screams at child.		1

77. Mother is made uncomfortable by child's
demonstration of affection.   1
78. Mother complains a lot about life.   1
79. Mother mandates child's play according to sex
(ie girls may only play with dolls).   1
80. Child is never allowed to make a mess.   1
81. Dolls are available to the child for play.   1

VIII Encouraging superego development
82. Mother expresses to the child her concern for
child's safety if there is a real danger.   1
83. There is a designated area for play.   1
84. Parents guard language in front of children.   1
85. Child is immediately spanked for running into the
street.   1
86. Mother mentions child asks questions showing
curiosity about how things work.   1
87. Child is taught to be respectful of adults.   1
88. Mother puts child to bed.   1
89. Mother mentions that she limits child's TV
watching.   1
90. Child is encouraged to care for own toys.   1
91. Child is taught to respect property of others.   1
92. Mother expresses pride in daughter's femininity
or son's masculinity.   1
93. Mother is able to show physical affection to child
comfortably.   1
94. There are books for adults in the house.   1
95. An effort is made to provide choices for the child. 1

IX Material giving
96. Crayons are made available to the child.   1
97. A play shovel is available to the child.   1
98. Child is sometimes rewarded for good behaviour
with a treat.   1
99. The child has a book of his own.   1

Definitions
The following definitions were used in making assessments:

A. Terms generally used
  1. *Appears* – is readily apparent from observation.
  2. *Complains* – expresses discontent with the situation.
  3. *Expresses* – reveals in any manner, as in words, gestures or actions.
  4. *Mentions* – spontaneous reference to.
  5. *Plans* – intentional ordering or arranging to achieve purpose or goal.

Seminar participants

The following people took part in the 'good-enough parenting' seminar from which these papers resulted. The seminar was held in September 1982 and the participants are listed here with descriptions of the posts they then held.

Speakers

Margaret Adcock	Principal Adviser, Education and Development, BAAF
Arnon Bentovim	Child and Family Psychiatrist, Hospital for Sick Children
Christine Cooper	Paediatrician, Newcastle-upon-Tyne
Richard White	Solicitor, BAAF

Participants

Yvonne Auger	Assistant Director and Child Care Adviser, London Borough of Lewisham
Roger Bacon	Researcher, Cambridge
Frank Bamford	Paediatrician, Manchester
Gill Gorell Barnes	Educational Consultant, Institute of Family Therapy
Liza Bingley	Social Worker, Hospital for Sick Children
Dora Black	Honorary Consultant Psychiatry, Hospital for Sick Children
Margaret Bryer	Member of BAAF Management Committee
Chris Butcher	Area Social Services Officer, London Borough of Lambeth
Russell Colburn	Director, Forest Heights Lodge, USA
Dr Anthony Cox	Maudsley Hospital, London
Christopher Dare	Psychiatrist, Maudsley Hospital
Cliff Davies	Lecturer in Psychology, University of Manchester
Fred Davies	Principal Social Worker in Child Care, Gloucestershire County Council
John Davies	Professor of Paediatrics, Addenbrooke's Hospital, Cambridge
Erica D'Eath	National Children's Bureau
Norman Dunning	Royal Scottish Society for the Prevention of Cruelty to Children
Chris Durrant	Senior Social Worker, Fostering and Adoption, Rochdale Borough Council